TABLE OF CONTENTS

ILLUSTRATIONS

CHAPTER 1: INTRODUCTION

Background of the Study

Over the past few decades Africa's volatile and complex environment has captured the attention of senior United States (U.S.) policy makers and Department of Defense (DOD) officials. The continent's emerging economy and marked increase in violent extremism particularly triggered the United States' interest in the mid 1990s. Correspondingly, Al-Qaeda's 1998 bombings of two U.S. embassies in East Africa coupled with their deadly attacks on September 11, 2001 marked a paradigm shift for the United States' strategic policy towards African affairs.[1] Al-Qaeda's use of African territories for coordinating global attacks forced the United States to realign priorities and place greater emphasis on neutralizing terrorist threats throughout the continent.[2]

Besides terrorism, in the early 2000s senior U.S. policy makers also became increasingly concerned with Africa for its natural resources and economic potential. Many American businesses were already involved in Africa and the continent's vast oil resources drew significant attention as a primary option for procurement of long term U.S. energy supplies. Therefore, in 2007, due to the region's growing geo-strategic importance President George W. Bush established a separate combatant command focused specifically on Africa.[3]

Since the U.S. Africa Command's (AFRICOM) formation in 2007, the organization has encountered numerous challenges. First, the command faces barriers interacting on the African continent due to its non-traditional design. AFRICOM has a headquarters in Germany; five

---

[1]David E. Brown, *AFRICOM at 5 Years: The Maturation of a New U.S. Combatant Command* (Carlisle, PA: Strategic Studies Institute, 2013), 4.

[2]Jeremy Keenan, *U.S. Militarization in Africa, Anthropology Today*, 24 (Oxford, England: Blackwell Publishing, 2008), 17.

[3]Brown, 5.

subordinate commands distributed throughout Europe, and one in the Horn of Africa.[4] The Combined Joint Task Force Horn of Africa (CJTF-HOA) in Djibouti is the only base AFRICOM has on African soil; therefore, the command conducts a large portion of planning and coordination of activities from its German headquarters. Consequently, AFRICOM experiences many difficulties in achieving unity of effort across the joint, interagency, intergovernmental, and multinational (JIIM) environment to enhance African stability and advance U.S. interests.

Additionally, unlike other combatant commands, AFRICOM's main purpose is not war fighting, but to develop and build partnerships for long-term national security. Upon its formation, the organization was given all the roles and responsibilities of a traditional combatant command but also a broader soft power mandate. The command is novel in the fact that it oversees traditional military activities and interagency programs that are funded through the State Department's budget.[5] AFRICOM's unique organizational structure seeks to facilitate a whole of government approach towards African affairs and better synchronize U.S. strategic efforts through unified action.

Therefore, AFRICOM's directed mission set focuses on leveraging and synchronizing all of the United States' instruments of national power for the strengthening of African defense capabilities, responding to African crises, and deterring transnational threats in order to advance U.S. national interests. The command is responsible for all DOD operations, exercises, and security cooperation in fifty-four nations on the African continent and its surrounding waters.[6]

Considering AFRICOM's distinctive charge and large operating area it has fewer resources than other combatant commands with similar requirements such as the U.S. Central

---

[4]Ibid, 19.

[5]Daniel Volman, "Why America wants a Military HQ in Africa," *New Africa* (January 2008): 37.

[6]Brown, 18.

Command (CENTCOM) and U.S. Pacific Command (PACOM). For example, the command does not have any assigned forces nor a dedicated theater sustainment command to accomplish its directed mission.

In addition to AFRICOM's unique design, novel responsibilities, and lack of resources, its operational environment also continues to increase in complexity. A large portion of North Africa is currently undergoing the Arab Spring movement, whereas East and Sub-Saharan Africa are experiencing a rise in Islamic extremism. Similarly, the entire continent routinely faces recurring civil wars, piracy, and disease. Considering AFRICOM's organizational structure and dynamic area of operations the command has performed well, consistently doing more with less. However, as problems in Africa continue to escalate and present additional threats to U.S. national security, the command may face issues it is not equipped or organizationally structured to negotiate.

One of these potential issues is the emerging threat on Africa's Oil Coast. As illustrated in Figure 1, this study defines the Oil Coast as the several countries bordering the Gulf of Guinea with a northern limit of Guinea-Bissau and southern boundary of Angola. Throughout the Oil Coast drug trafficking, transnational crime, and terrorism are fomenting major problem sets. The illegal smuggling of narcotics from Oil Coast countries such as Guinea-Bissau is adversely impacting many countries throughout Africa, Europe, and North America. In addition, the region is becoming another sanctuary for Islamic Extremism. The rise of Boko Haram in Nigeria, coupled with the growing influence of Al-Qaeda and Al-Shabaab threatens to provoke further issues in the area. Islamic Extremism, corruption, and lack of government transparency on the Oil Coast also endanger the region's lucrative oil and energy industries. A large number of African and international and businesses are regularly facing hazards from various non-state actors, which jeopardize the obtainment of future energy resources, stability of the world's oil market, and global commerce.

Figure 1. Map of Africa's Oil Coast
Source: University of Texas Austin, http://www.lib.utexas.edu/maps/africa/africa_pol95.jpg
(accessed 30 November 2013).

Holistically, the interdependent issues on Africa's Oil Coast threaten long-term
continental security and jeopardize U.S. interests. The combination of the aforementioned issues
have manifested into an arc of instability that could have future strategic implications. Since
2007, AFRICOM has continuously adapted to its rapidly changing operational environment. The
organization has achieved positive results with finite resources. However, given the critical state
of African affairs and potential impact on American interests, senior U.S. policy makers should
consider re-assessing where and how to most effectively focus the instruments of national power.
Senior U.S. policy makers and DOD officials should contemplate re-framing the African
operational environment and examine options that could more efficiently facilitate the linkage of
tactical actions to strategic ends across both time and space. One prospective operational
approach is to place more emphasis and resources towards stabilizing Africa's Oil Coast.

Overall, due to the vast complexity and rising potential for conflict in Africa this study examines AFRICOM's organizational structure and ability to protect vital U.S. national interests. Also, the researcher highlights the growing geo-strategic importance of the African continent and it's Oil Coast. The researcher's working hypothesis for the study is that given the current state of African affairs, AFRICOM lacks a sufficient organizational structure and resources to accomplish its mission set, specifically on the Oil Coast. Additionally, failure to overlook the Oil Coast's aforementioned problem sets will present strategic implications and operational challenges in the anticipated global environment.

Statement of the Problem

Since the U.S. Africa Command's (AFRICOM) formation in 2007, the organization has encountered numerous challenges. First, the command has limited access to its area of operations. AFRICOM's only subordinate command located on the African continent is CJTF-HOA.[7] Therefore, acquiring an accurate assessment of African affairs and achieving unity of effort across the JIIM environment is difficult. Furthermore, accomplishing the command's non-traditional mission set and broader soft power mandate with limited resources is a complicated task. AFRICOM's operational environment also continues to increase in volatility and complexity. A large portion of North Africa is undergoing the Arab Spring movement, whereas East and Sub-Saharan Africa are experiencing a rise in Islamic extremism. Congruently, the entire continent routinely faces recurring civil wars, piracy, and disease.

As AFRICOM continues to focus resources and stability efforts in Eastern and Northern Africa, there is a new set of emerging threats on Africa's Oil Coast which directly affect vital U.S. interests. The rise of Al-Qaeda in the lands of the Maghreb (AQIM) and Nigerian based

---

[7]Brown, 19.

Boko Haram threaten African and international prosperity. The violent extremist organizations' (VEO) illicit trafficking and escalating attacks on critical infrastructure jeopardize global security and commerce.[8]

Therefore, as the African continent continues to manifest instability does AFRICOM have the right organizational structure to build African defense capacity, deter transnational threats, promote continental stability, and protect U.S. national interests? Additionally, given the current state of African affairs, where should AFRICOM prioritize its resources to gain a position of relative advantage in the anticipated operational environment?

Purpose of the Study

This study has two distinct purposes. The first purpose is to highlight the importance of Africa's Oil Coast and that the regions emerging threats require greater attention from senior U.S. policy makers and DOD officials. The second purpose is to examine AFRICOM's organizational structure and assess the command's organizational effectiveness, specifically on the Oil Coast.

Significance of the Study

This study is significant because there is a lack of empirical research on AFRICOM's organizational structure and ability to accomplish its directed mission set and desired end state. In addition, the study highlights how the Oil Coast is increasing in strategic importance and threatens long-term U.S. interests. The results of this study will provide senior-level decision makers with another prospective regarding the strategic importance of Africa's Oil Coast. Additionally, the researcher illustrates some of AFRICOM's structural shortfalls that can be used

---

[8]Femi Adegbulu, "From Guerrilla Tactics to Outright Terrorism: A Study of Boko Haram's Synergy with Al-Qaeda Terrorist Network," *The IUP Journal of International Relations*, 7, no. 2, (2013): 80.

to adapt its organizational design. Furthermore, the information from this study provides critical insights regarding potential friction points when structuring combatant commands for the anticipated operational environment.

Theoretical Framework

Several theoretical frameworks are included in this study. For examination of AFRICOM's organizational structure the researcher referenced organizational theory. More specifically this study analyzed four sub-components of organizational theory: what is an organization, an organization as an open system, organizational design, and organizational effectiveness. Additionally, the researcher incorporated systems theory to assess the emerging threats on Oil Coast. Systems theory helped the researcher gain an understanding of the region, its actors, and their relationships. Overall, the aforementioned frameworks provided the foundation for this entire study.

Research Questions

The major question guiding this study was to examine if the complexity and strategic importance of Africa's Oil Coast will present operational problems for AFRICOM as currently constructed. The four specific research questions addressed were:

1. Do the emerging threats on Africa's Oil Coast threaten long-term U.S. interests and global stability?

2. Does AFRICOM have a sufficient organizational structure and capabilities to deter emerging threats throughout the continent, specifically on Africa's Oil Coast?

3. Does AFRICOM have sufficient forces and allocated resources to facilitate linkage of tactical actions with strategic ends throughout its area of operations?

4. Given the unique design of AFRICOM and its geographic challenges, is the organization effectively accomplishing its key tasks and desired end state throughout Africa, specifically its Oil Coast?

Limitations

The primary limitations for this study are that the researcher was unable to physically observe and examine AFRICOM's organizational structure and assess its effectiveness. Therefore, the researcher had to rely on scholarly data and information gathered from personal interviews of AFRICOM staff members. Finally, the scope of the researcher's interviews was limited to select personnel and information obtained could vary based on individual biases, situational understanding, and expertise.

Assumptions

This study includes three assumptions. First, that the scholarly data used for analysis was accurate regarding the emerging threats on Africa's Oil Coast and AFRICOM's organizational structure. Second, that the selected interviewees responded to the researcher's questions in an honest and unbiased manner. Finally, the researcher assumes that the interpretation of scholarly data and interviews correctly reflects the perceptions of the various authors and participants.

Organization of the Study

This research study consists of five chapters. Chapter I includes the background of the study, statement of the problem, purpose of the study, significance of the study, theoretical framework, research questions, limitations, and assumptions of the study. Chapter II presents a review of literature, which focuses on organizational theory and systems theory. Chapter III describes the methodology used for this study and includes the selection of data collection and data analysis procedures. Chapter IV presents the main body of the study and highlights how the emerging threats on Africa's Oil Coast will impact several American and global interests. In addition, Chapter IV presents a case study on AFRICOM's organizational structure and the command's effectiveness, specifically on the Oil Coast. Finally, Chapter V provides a summary of the entire study and recommendations.

CHAPTER II: LITERATURE REVIEW

Introduction

The following review of literature provides a brief discussion of key concepts pertinent to this research study. The researcher examined a variety of theoretical frameworks to gain a holistic understanding of AFRICOM and its operational environment. Furthermore, detailed analysis of organizational theory and systems theory provided the researcher a broad foundation to identify potential friction points within AFRICOM's organizational structure and the challenges associated with the threats on Africa's Oil Coast.

Organizational Theory

The primary theoretical framework for this study is organizational theory. More specifically, to gain a comprehensive understanding of AFRICOM's organizational construct this study incorporates three sub-components of organizational theory: an organization as an open system, organizational structure, and organizational effectiveness. Given the various challenges that a modern organization faces, analysis of several contemporary theorists' concepts enabled the researcher to become familiar with AFRICOM's organizational design. As AFRICOM continues to explore options for achieving a position of relative advantage throughout its operational environment, examination of the command's organizational structure is critical. Therefore, this study uses existing literature to assess AFRICOM's current organizational configuration and evaluate its operational effectiveness.

Understanding the definition of an organization and the characteristics of an open system provided a framework to analyze AFRICOM's organizational design. Furthermore, it allowed the researcher to examine AFRICOM's current configuration and desired outputs. From a theoretical perspective, "An organization is a coordinated social entity, which functions on a relatively continuous basis to achieve a common goal or set of goals."[9] Organizations exist when people interact with one another to perform essential functions, which are linked to the external environment.[10] An organization's external environment is defined as all elements that exist outside the boundary of an organization that can potentially affect all or part of the organization.[11]

In order to understand, visualize, and describe AFRICOM's structure and external environment the researcher incorporated organizational theorist Richard Daft's open system framework. An open system model recognizes that organizations are complex and must continuously interact and adapt to its external environment.[12] An open system is an arrangement of interrelated and interacting components of an organization with its external environment to achieve common objectives. Essentially an open system acquires inputs from the environment, transforms them, and discharges outputs to the external environment.[13]

The open system framework, visually depicted in Figure 2, provided the researcher a valuable tool to comprehend AFRICOM's internal architecture, its functions and processes, and how the command acts throughout the operational environment. Analysis of Daft's open system framework facilitated the researchers understanding of AFRICOM's internal functions and

---

[9]Stephen P. Robbins, *Organization Theory: Structure, Design, and Applications* (Englewood Cliffs, NJ: Prentice-Hill, 1990), 4.

[10]Richard L. Daft, *Organization Theory and Design*, 7th ed. (Cincinnati, OH: South-Western Educational Publishing/Thomson, 2001), 12.

[11]Ibid., 130.

[12]Ibid., 14.

[13]Ibid.

interaction throughout its external environment. However, to obtain a more in depth appreciation for AFRICOM's configuration and organizational structure, the researcher referenced several of Mary Jo Hatch's design templates.

Figure 2. An Open System and its Subsystems
Source: Richard L. Daft, *Organization Theory and Design*, 7th ed. (Cincinnati, OH: South-Western Educational Publishing/Thomson, 2001), 12.

Hatch and many contemporary theorists posit that an organization's structure should reflect the conditions it faces in its environment.[14] Hatch describes organizational design as the process of continuously adapting organizational structures and processes to enhance performance.[15] Organizational design is effective if it guides the various activities of employees and promotes ease of integration across all organizational functions. Furthermore, the design is efficient if it minimizes time, effort, and resources needed to achieve organizational goals.[16]

Throughout this study, the researcher examined three of Mary Jo Hatch's basic design templates to assess AFRICOM's current configuration and efficiency. The first template that the

---

[14]Paul R. Lawrence and Jay W. Lorsch, *Organization and Environment* (Boston: Harvard Business Press, 1967), 8-13.

[15]Mary Jo Hatch and Ann L. Cunliffe, *Organization Theory: Modern, Symbolic, and Postmodern Perspectives*, 2nd ed. (New York: Oxford University Press, USA, 2006), 296.

[16]Ibid.

researcher referenced is a multi-divisional design. A multidivisional form is a set of functionally structured units that report to a headquarters staff. The management of each functionally structured unit is responsible for their internal operations, while the organizational headquarters is responsible for the long-range strategic development of the institution.[17] Multidivisional form organizations group functional units by geographic region or similarities in products and processes. As highlighted in Figure 3, this design gives organizations a competitive advantage in size and footprint, which facilitates greater influence throughout their external environment. AFRICOM's current organizational design is generally a multidivisional form.

Figure 3. An Organizational Chart Showing a Multidivisional Design.
Source: Mary Jo Hatch and Ann L. Cunliffe, *Organization Theory: Modern, Symbolic, and Postmodern Perspectives*, 2nd ed. (New York: Oxford University Press, USA, 2006), 296.

Another type of design the researcher evaluated is the matrix configuration. Essentially a matrix design, as illustrated in Figure 4, has two interacting structures. A functional component that provides individual specialization and a project side which pools together functional experts across the entire organization to complete a given task. The matrix provides a balanced organizational design that maximizes vertical control and efficiency with the collaboration of a

---

[17]Hatch and Cunliffe, 296.

horizontal learning structure. Additionally, it enables more flexibility and adaptability for reaction to emerging problem sets than other design templates.[18]

Hatch's two aforementioned organizational design templates represent pure types. Organizations will not always conform to these exact models. Another design template is a hybrid framework that provides combinations of the multi-divisional and matrix configurations to gain a competitive advantage. Most large companies today, utilize a hybrid construct to allow flexibility and adaptability within subunits due to rapidly changing environments.

Figure 4. Two Examples of an Organizational Chart Showing a Matrix Design.
Source: Mary Jo Hatch and Ann L. Cunliffe, *Organization Theory: Modern, Symbolic, and Postmodern Perspectives*, 2nd ed. (New York: Oxford University Press, USA, 2006), 296.

Another critical component included within all of the aforementioned structural design templates is an organization's dynamic network structure. The current impact of globalization has yielded significant increases in technology that is helping to improve internal and external organizational communication. Therefore, organizations such as AFRICOM must weigh the

---

[18]Ibid., 302-306.

benefits of investing and building a robust network structure. Advances in information technology and the network are enabling organizations to become smaller while simultaneously extending operational reach, decentralize organizational activities, and improve horizontal and vertical information flow throughout their environment.

Richard Daft and Mary Jo Hatch's frameworks provided the researcher with a theoretical foundation to comprehend AFRICOM's current organizational structure, functions and processes. However, to assess the combatant command's ability to accomplish its mission and desired end state, the researcher analyzed several approaches to measuring organizational effectiveness. Theorist Amitai Etzioni defines organizational effectiveness as the "degree to which an organization achieves its goals" and as "a desired state of affairs which the organization attempts to realize."[19] Assessing organizational effectiveness is very complex and no standard measure will provide an unequivocal assessment of performance. Therefore, for this study the researcher analyzed four common theoretical frameworks used to assess organizational effectiveness known as the goal-based approach, resource-based approach, internal process approach, and stakeholders approach.

The goal-based approach defines effectiveness in terms of outputs and how well an organization accomplishes its goals.[20] The resource-based approach claims that effectiveness is attained to the extent that the organization acquires the necessary inputs or valued resources to carry out its purpose.[21] In the stakeholder approach, the satisfaction of any group within or outside an organization is evaluated through individual criterion as an indicator of the organization's performance.[22] Lastly, the internal processes approach measures effectiveness as

---

[19]Amitai Etzioni, *Modern Organizations* (Englewood Cliffs, NJ: Prentice-Hall, 1964), 6.

[20]Hodge, Anthony, and Gales, 75.

[21]Ibid., 76.

[22]Ibid., 69.

internal organizational health and efficiency or the efficient use of resources and harmonious internal functioning.[23]

Systems Theory

Systems theory helped the researcher examine the emerging threats on Africa's Oil Coast. More specifically, the theoretical construct provided a framework to gain an appreciation of the region and its actors. Systems theory analyzes the relationships of its members to one another and to the whole. Jamshid Gharajedaghi contends that seeing the whole requires understanding a systems structure, functions, processes, and content. Structure defines the components or actors and their relationships; function defines the outcomes or results produced; process is the sequence of activities and know-how required to produce outcomes; and content defines the unique environment in which the system is situated.[24] Overall, gaining an appreciation of systems theory allowed the researcher to explore Africa's current operational environment, specifically the relationships and interactions of actors on Africa's Oil Coast.

Literature Review Summary

Overall, the examination of literature from several scholars on organizational theory and systems theory provided a holistic framework to assess AFRICOM's current configuration and the emerging threats on Africa's Oil Coast. Understanding the basic definition and underlying functions of an organization provided a contextual basis for analyzing AFRICOM's organizational architecture. Furthermore, comprehension of an organization as an open system facilitated the researchers understanding of AFRICOM's internal functions and interactions throughout its external environment. Mary Jo Hatch also highlighted several design templates to

---

[23]Ibid., 68.

[24]Jamshid Gharajedaghi. *Systems Thinking: Managing Chaos and Complexity: A Platform for Designing Business Architecture*, 2nd ed (New York: Elsevier, 2006), 110.

improve organizational efficiency and effectiveness based on a certain environment and its conditions. Finally, systems theory allowed the researcher to explore Africa's current operational environment, specifically the relationships and interactions of actors on Africa's Oil Coast.

CHAPTER III: METHODOLOGY

To answer the primary research question regarding how the complexity and strategic importance of Africa's Oil Coast will present operational problems for AFRICOM as currently constructed, this monograph uses a process tracing methodology. As adopted by former RAND Corporation analyst Alexander George, process tracing involves the historical examination of problems, to identify conditions associated with either successful or failed outcomes.[25] The goal of such historical explanations is to determine if a causal process is evident.[26]

Data Collection

The researcher collected data for this monograph utilizing three qualitative methods. The first method consisted of gathering a large amount of scholarly data and documentary research. The consolidation of literature was screened for validity and specifically examined organizational theory, AFRICOM as an organization, and information regarding the strategic importance and emerging threats on Africa's Oil Coast. The second method included a specific case study on AFRICOM's organizational structure and effectiveness. The third method incorporated the use of elite interviewing to corroborate information from the researcher's sources of literature and case study. The researcher conducted interviews through a non-random sampling technique comprised of two approaches: convenience sampling and homogenous sampling. The interview participants consisted of several senior Department of Defense (DOD) employees and military officers from

---

[25]Andrew Bennett and Alexander L. George, *Case Studies and Theory Development in the Social Science* (Cambridge, MA: MIT Press, 2005), 5.

[26]Ibid., 6.

AFRICOM, a battalion commander from the 2nd Armored Brigade Combat Team (ABCT), 1st Infantry Division (ID) and an interagency representative. In general, the interviewees provided an elite sample of experienced individuals to make further inferences.

Data Analysis

The qualitative data consolidated in this study was analyzed through two methods. The first method consisted of comparing existing literature with the responses from elite interviews. The interviewees' responses were compared against each other for internal consistency, then alongside existing research regarding AFRICOM's organizational structure and effectiveness. The second method included a congruence procedure between the consolidated literature, elite interviews, and AFRICOM case study.[27] Overall, the aforementioned analysis of data ultimately led to the researcher's recommendations and conclusions.

CHAPTER IV: DATA ANALYSIS

Why Africa's Oil Coast?

As Africa continues to become more complex, the United States and its combatant command AFRICOM should consider focusing more efforts toward reducing the growing arc of instability on the continents Oil Coast. The region's rise in violent extremist activities, illicit drug trafficking, and lucrative oil resources represent vital and interdependent subjects that directly affect long-term American national interests. AFRICOM's continental focus on capacity building and deterrence of transnational threats is yielding positive impacts; however, as the Oil Coast becomes more volatile and complex the command should contemplate reframing its operational environment. The challenges associated with Al-Shabaab and South Sudan in East Africa coupled with the Arab Spring movements in North Africa has drawn most of AFRICOM's attention.

---

[27]Stephen Van Evera, *Guide to Methods for Students of Political Science* (Ithaca: Cornell University Press, 1997), 58-60.

However, a failure to overlook the manifestation of threats throughout the Oil Coast could have grave consequences.

Africa's Oil Coast is very important to U.S. interests and its efforts to counter violent extremist organizations. President Obama highlights countering terrorism and the defeat of Al-Qaeda or its affiliates as the core concern of the United States.[28] As previously mentioned, two major Al-Qaeda affiliates are prominent in Africa, Al-Shabaab in the East and Al-Qaeda in the Lands of the Islamic Maghreb (AQIM) in the Northwest. Recent efforts in the East through the African Union's mission in Somalia (AMISOM) and CJTF-HOA have moderately impacted Al-Shabaab. However, AQIM has not received the same amount of pressure. In his 2013 posture statement, former AFRICOM commander General Carter Ham identified AQIM as the most likely near-term threat to U.S. interests. In the aftermath of the Arab Spring movements in Libya and Tunisia, AQIM has spread its footprint and influence from Algeria into Mali, Niger, and the uncontested Sahel region.[29] The organization's operational reach and capacity has steadily increased threatening to de-stabilize countries within Africa's Oil Coast.

AQIM became a legitimate Al-Qaeda affiliate in 2006. Since the merger, AQIM's targeting and tactics broadened significantly. Beginning in 2007, AQIM carried out more frequent and more sophisticated attacks such as the bombings on United Nations (UN) offices in Algiers, Algeria killing sixty people.[30] In addition, as illustrated in Figure 5, from 2007-2012 AQIM attacks spread beyond Algeria to several neighboring states, reflecting the organization's new

---

[28]President Barack Obama, *Sustaining US Global Leadership: Priorities for the 21st Century* (Washington DC: Government Printing Office, 2012), 4.

[29]Ham, 8.

[30]Jonathan Masters, "Al-Qaeda in the Islamic Maghreb (AQIM)," *Council on Foreign Relations* (2013): 1-2, http://www.cfr.org/world/al-qaeda-islamic-maghreb-aqim/p12717 (accessed 27 December 2013).

ambition for forging a regional Islamist caliphate rather than simply imposing sharia law in Algeria alone.

The spread of AQIM's presence from North Africa into Mali, Niger, and the uncontested Sahel region present formidable threats to continental security. AQIM's establishment of basing and recruitment sites in these areas is undermining long-term regional stability efforts which are spilling over into the Oil Coast. The organization's guerilla-style raids, assassinations, and suicide bombings of military, government, and civilian targets coupled with their array of criminal activities such as kidnappings for ransom and drug trafficking present several challenges.[31] Due to the ungoverned space AQIM operates in, its criminal activities are extremely successful yielding substantial monetary gains.

Figure 5. Spread of AQIM Attacks from 2007-2012
Source: Jonathan Masters, Al-Qaeda in the Islamic Maghreb (AQIM)," *Council on Foreign Relations* (2013): 1-2, http://www.cfr.org/world/al-qaeda-islamic-maghreb-aqim/p12717 (accessed 27 December 2013).

---

[31]U.S. Department of State, *2012 Country Reports on Terrorism* (Washington, DC: Government Printing Office), 264.

AQIM's lucrative economic base makes them a significant threat on Africa's Oil Coast. The organization can conduct terrorist attacks or provide funding and equipment in support of rebel factions seeking to de-stabilize pro-democratic governments such as the Tuareg's in Northern Mali.[32] With regional instability, AQIM may leverage the opportunity to expand its operations along the southern Sahelian axis to Africa's Oil Coast and mount attacks on western targets in the region. Furthermore, AQIM's potential merger with other local extremist groups such as Nigerian based Boko Haram, presents several challenges that could manifest wide spread violence and create another safe haven for Al-Qaeda's global jihad to train, recruit, and stage attacks against the United States and Europe.[33]

In addition to AQIM, another terrorist organization labeled Boko Haram poses significant threats to Oil Coast nations and long-term U.S. interests. Boko Haram established itself in 2002 to reject the authority of the Nigerian state, western-style education, secular governance, and any religious interpretations of Islam that run counter to its teachings.[34] From 2009 to the present day Boko Haram has steadily increased its operations and influence. In recent years, the organization has exploited the perceived corruption of the Nigerian government and growing economic disparity between Nigeria's predominantly Christian south and Muslim north.[35] Capitalizing on this narrative, the group has drawn support from several thousand Nigerians, primarily young

---

[32]Masters, 1-2.

[33]Christopher S. Chivvis and Andrew Liepman, *North Africa's Menace: AQIM's Evolution and the U.S. Policy Response* (Santa Monica, CA: RAND Corporation, 2013), 7-8. http://www.rand.org/pubs/research_reports/RR415/ (accessed 27 December 2013).

[34]Qatar International Academy for Security Studies, *2012 Countering Violent Extremist Report* (September 2013), 171.

[35]Ibid., 172.

men from the northeast, who have expressed frustration with the lack of development, jobs, and investment in the north.[36]

Since 2009, Boko Haram has utilized this support to launch more sophisticated and larger scale attacks. Recent crises in Libya and Egypt have facilitated their smuggling and obtainment of explosive devices, weapons, and refurbished shoulder fired surface to air missiles.[37] Correspondingly, Boko Haram's attacks have increased in frequency, reach, and lethality, now occurring almost daily in northeast Nigeria, and periodically beyond.[38] The organization has expanded operations from small-scale ambushes on local security forces to mass-casualty suicide bombings predominately targeting civilians.[39] During the first four months of 2013, Boko Haram matched its total number of suicide attacks from 2012, engaging in at least sixteen different operations targeting Christian churches, police stations, local newspaper offices, and government buildings killing or wounding hundreds.[40] In addition to bombings, the group has significantly amplified its criminal activities. Recently bank robberies have become a prominent Boko Haram operation. In 2011, Nigeria had over 100 bank robberies, thirty of which the extremist organization claimed directly. These robberies continue to grow and severely threaten Nigerian

---

[36]Lauren Ploch, "Nigeria: Current Issues and U.S. Policy," *Congressional Research Service* (April 2013): 13, https://www.fas.org/sgp/crs/row/RL33964.pdf/ (accessed 28 December 2013).

[37]David Ignatius, "Libyan missiles on the loose," *Washington Post*, 8 May 2012, http://www.washingtonpost.com/opinions/libyan-missiles-on-theloose/2012/05/08/gIQA1FCUBU_story.html/ (accessed 29 December 2013).

[38]Ploch, "Nigeria: Current Issues and U.S. Policy," Congressional Research Service, 13.

[39]"Boko Haram: An Increasingly Radical Threat," *Soufan Group* (19 June 2012): 2, http://soufangroup.com/tsg-intelbrief-boko-haram-an-increasingly-radical-threat/?catid=3/ (accessed 28 December 2013).

[40]U.S. House of Representatives Committee on Homeland Services, "Boko Haram: Growing Threat to the U.S. Homeland," (13 September 2013): 18, http://homeland.house.gov/sites/ homeland.house.gov/files/documents/09-13-13-Boko-Haram-Report.pdf/ (accessed 28 December 2013).

prosperity as one of Africa's top economic countries and significant trade partner with the United States.[41]

Similarly, Boko Haram continues to expand its kidnapping operations of Western civilians for ransom sums to areas such as Cameroon.[42] Holistically, Boko Haram has become a serious threat to the region and American interests. According to former U.S. Assistant Secretary of State for African Affairs Johnnie Carson, "Boko Haram has created widespread insecurity across northern Nigeria, increased tensions between various ethnic communities, interrupted development activities, frightened off investors, and generated concerns among Nigeria's northern neighbors. Through these activities, it is the goal of Boko Haram to humiliate and undermine the government and to exploit religious differences in order to create chaos and to make Nigeria ungovernable."[43] Additionally, speaking at the George Washington University's Homeland Security Policy Institute in December 2012, former AFRICOM Commander General Carter Ham compared Boko Haram's status to that of Al Qaeda in the 1990s and highlighted the group's potential to extend operations internationally.[44]

Another significant concern throughout Africa's Oil Coast is the growing synergy and partnerships between violent extremist organizations such as AQIM and Boko Haram. In January 2010, AQIM formally announced that it would assist Boko Haram with training, personnel, and

---

[41]The Jamestown Foundation, "Instability in Nigeria: The Domestic Factors," (19 June 2012): 3, https://www.cimicweb.org/cmo/compapp/Documents/docExchange/ Instability_in_Nigeria-Boko_Haram_Conference_Report.pdf/ (accessed 28 December 2013).

[42]"Nigeria's Boko Haram 'got $3m ransom' to Free Hostages," *BBC News*, 26 April, 2013, http://www.bbc.co.uk/news/world-africa-22320077/ (accessed 28 December 2013).

[43]Johnnie Carson, Assistant Secretary of State for African Affairs Nigeria, "One Year After Elections," (9 April 2012): 2, http://www.state.gov/p/af/rls/rm/2012/187721.htm/ (accessed 28 December 2013).

[44]General Carter Ham, "Counterterrorism in Africa," speech at The Homeland Security Policy Institute, 3 December 2012, 10, http://www.gwumc.edu/hspi/events/ GENHamPRF416.cfm/ (accessed 28 December 2013).

equipment.[45] International pressure on AQIM operations in North Africa triggered the organization to search for additional safe havens in Africa's Sahel region. In exchange for training Boko Haram offered AQIM operating space in Northeastern Nigeria and adjacent regions.[46] The lack of security and ungoverned space of the Sahel and Northern Nigeria facilitate freedom of maneuver for these extremist organizations' to collaborate and train. AQIM has recently set up training camps in Niger, Northern Mali, and Mauritania in which Boko Haram members have attended.[47] Additionally, the unregulated and crime polluted Sahel region offers the groups opportunities to combine finances and resources for future attacks. A likely course of action would be for the two organizations to conduct attacks on Nigeria's Oil industry which is of significant concern to U.S. and global interests. Furthermore, the groups could launch coordinated operations against Western targets and regional pro-democratic governments. Finally, the potential synchronization of AQIM operations in the Northwest, Boko Haram attacks throughout Oil Coast, and the acts of piracy in the Gulf of Guinea would have catastrophic effects throughout the continent and global environment.

AFRICOM recognizes the complexity associated with violent extremist activity on Africa's Oil Coast and has taken some initial steps to deter these growing threats. The command's annual Flintlock exercise, facilitated by Special Operations Command Africa, fosters regional cooperation improving the military capacities of select African partners to counter violent extremism and increase regional stability[48] Additionally, AFRICOM's participation in the

---

[45]U.S. House of Representatives Committee on Homeland Services, "Boko Haram: Growing Threat to the U.S. Homeland," (30 November 2011): 20, http://homelandhouse.gov /sites/homeland.house.gov/files/boko%20haram-%20emerging%20Threat%20to%20the %20US%20Homeland.pdf/ (accessed 28 December 2013).

[46]Ibid.

[47]Adegbulu, 80.

[48]U.S. African Command, *Flintlock Exercise*, http://www.africom.mil/what-we-do/exercises/flintlock/ (accessed 29 December 2013).

Department of State's (DOS) African Contingency and Training Assistance (ACOTA) program is slowly enhancing several Oil Coast countries militaries' capabilities through additional training and equipment.[49] However, these activities have not been enough to reduce conflict or disrupt violent extremist activities throughout the Oil Coast. As AQIM and Boko Haram continue to escalate attacks and rise in prominence additional options require consideration before the region experiences chaos. AFRICOM commander, General David Rodriguez made an interesting comment in his October 2013 interview on LiveAtState regarding U.S. Foreign Policy in Sub-Saharan Africa, stating "AFRICOM will continue looking for opportunities to better coordinate our strategy with multinational and our interagency partners, and we will align our resources with our strategy and do our very best to ensure we are applying our efforts where they are most effective and most needed."[50] Considering General Rodriguez' narrative, a potential option for the command to consider is reviewing its continental priorities and placing more emphasis on countering violent extremism and other threats on Africa's Oil Coast.

A primary source of funding for a violent extremist organization such as AQIM or Boko Haram is illicit drug trafficking. Congruently, since 2004 Africa's Oil Coast has emerged as a major transit point for cocaine and other illegal drugs from South America and Asia. The region's lack of governance, porous land and maritime borders and lack of maritime interdiction assets has made Africa's Oil Coast the epicenter of the world drug trade.[51] The flow of cocaine through the Oil Coast and West Africa peaked in 2007 when forty-seven tons of cocaine flowed through the

---

[49]U.S. African Command, *African Contingency Operations Training and Assistance Fact Sheet*, http://www.africom.mil/what-we-do/ (accessed 29 December 2013).

[50]U.S. African Command, "Transcript: General Rodriguez on Security Cooperation in Sub-Saharan Africa," (25 October 2013): 1-2, http://www.africom.mil/ Newsroom/ Transcript/11406/general-rodriguez-on-security-cooperation-in-sub-saharan-africa/ (accessed 29 December 2013).

[51]Liana Wyler and Nicolas Cook, "Drug Trafficking in West Africa: Background and Possible Questions for an Upcoming Hearing," *Congressional Research Service* (8 May 2012): 1.

region. The cocaine smuggling dropped to eighteen tons in 2010, which still amounts to $1.25 billion in wholesale revenue. This lucrative industry poses significant threats to U.S. interests. The fact that extremist organizations such as AQIM and Boko Haram have access to such large sums of finances is alarming. Especially considering that the military budgets for most Oil Coast countries is less than the wholesale price of a ton of cocaine.[52] Furthermore, drug trafficking is significantly contributing to lack of government transparency and instability throughout the region.

The United Nations Office on Drugs and Crime (UNODC) describes the Oil Coast and West Africa as "under attack from within and especially from abroad."[53] Narcotics trafficking and other illegal activities are undermining the legitimacy and effectiveness of many Oil Coast governments and stunting their economic development. Illicit drug trafficking and criminal activities are increasing the regions potential for internal conflicts. Furthermore, they are deterring outside investment and promoting inflation, negating several countries' sustainable development practices and abilities to promote their citizens well-being.[54] A prime example is the country of Guinea-Bissau on the northern tip of Africa's Oil Coast.

Once viewed as a potential model for African development, Guinea-Bissau is currently Africa's most fragile state and is the main transit point for illicit drug trafficking throughout the Oil Coast and West Africa.[55] Thirteen percent of the world's cocaine flow is trafficked through

---

[52]United Nations Office on Drugs and Crime, Transnational Organized Crime in West Africa: A Threat Assessment (February 2013), 1, 4.

[53]United Nations Office of Drugs and Crime, Transnational Trafficking and the Rule of Law in West Africa: A Threat Assessment (Vienna 2009), 1.

[54]U.S. Government, Interagency Strategy, *West Africa Cooperative Security Initiative (WACSI)* (Washington, DC: Government Printing Office, 2011), 5.

[55]The Africa Center for Strategic Studies, "Advancing Stability and Reconciliation in Guinea-Bissau: Lessons from Africa's First Narco-State," (June 2013): 1.

Guinea-Bissau.[56] The UNODC estimates that thirty to thirty-five tons of cocaine is trafficked through the country annually.[57] Guinea-Bissau's current situation is the result of decades of political turmoil. Democracy has failed to take hold because of the centralization of government power, corruption, and weak internal security forces. The flow of cocaine through the country is a key contributor to the instability and has increasingly led to their isolation by the international community.[58] Although not as severe, the underlying problems within Guinea-Bissau are present within most Oil Coast countries. Additionally, the synergistic effects and growing influence of extremist organizations throughout the region further magnifies the scope of this problem, which could manifest major issues for the African continent and global community.

The DOS and AFRICOM understand the problems associated with drug trafficking and violent extremism throughout Africa's Oil Coast. Furthermore, that these activities threaten the collective security and regional stability interests of the United States, its African partners, and the international community. In 2011 the DOS launched the West African Cooperative Security Initiative (WACSI) which was specifically designed to improve several African Oil Coast nations' abilities to combat organized crime, specifically drug trafficking.[59] Through a whole of government approach in consultation with African and international partners, the DOS sought to leverage unity of effort to deter this growing threat. WACSI is a five-year plan focused on increasing the capacity of several Oil Coast nations through building accountable institutions,

---

[56]William Brownfield, Assistant Security of State for International Narcotics and Law Enforcement Affairs, testimony before the Senate Caucus on International Narcotics Control, 12 March 2013.

[57]The United Nations Office on Drugs and Crime, Transnational Organized Crime in West Africa: A Threat Assessment, February 2012, 9.

[58]Ibid.

[59]U.S. Government, West Africa Cooperative Security Initiative (WACSI), 5.

establishing legal and policy frameworks, strengthening security operations, reinforcing justice

operations and addressing the socio-economic causes of organized crime.[60]

AFRICOM plays a significant role in the WACSI program. The command has

established a Counter Narco-Terrorism and Law Enforcement Assistance Division (CN-LEA) to

help reduce the flow of drugs throughout Africa to the United States, Europe, the Middle East and

Asia. CN-LEA builds the counternarcotics capacity of African partner nations to combat

narcotics, control their borders and increase interdiction on land and at sea. CN-LEA capacity

building projects involve over two dozen African countries, but primary efforts are concentrated

in West Africa and the Trans-Sahara region.[61] Currently, AFRICOM's main effort for deterring

transnational crime and drug trafficking is West Africa and the Oil Coast. CN-LEA's annual

twenty million dollar budget for West Africa does not go far; however, AFRICOM utilizes its

limited resources to conduct small scale exercises and training with willing and able countries.[62]

Due to ample means, WACSI is designed to prioritize funding and assistance to designated

anchor states that have demonstrated both the will and the capability to partner with the United

States to combat organized crime. Presently, the Oil Coast states of Ghana and Nigeria receive

the majority of WACSI assistance due their recent efforts and commitment to countering illicit

trafficking.[63]

In conjunction with WACSI, AFRICOM should consider re-looking its current

operational approach to layer effects throughout Africa's Oil Coast in anchor states such as

---

[60]U.S. Department of State: Bureau of International Narcotics and Law Enforcement Affairs, *The West Africa Cooperative Security Initiative: A Shared Partnership*, (3 July 2012): 1, http://www.state.gov/documents/organization/166329.pdf/ (accessed 2 January 2014).

[61]Amon Killeen, U.S. Africa Command (USAFRICOM) Counter Narco-Terrorism and Law Enforcement Assistance Division (USAFRICOM: 30 September 2013), 1-2.

[62]Mark Huebschman, Deputy Chief, Counter Narcotics and Law Enforcement Division, J5, US AFRICOM, interviewed by author, Fort Leavenworth, Kansas, 17 December 2013.

[63]U.S. Government, West Africa Cooperative Security Initiative (WACSI), 7-8.

Nigeria and Ghana. As shown in Figure 6, countering violent extremism and illicit trafficking are interdependent. Therefore, if the command truly wants to find optimal ways to align its resources and strategy to effectively apply efforts, then a potential option is to make Africa's Oil Coast their decisive operation. Due to the growing influence and threat of the aforementioned violent extremist organizations in the region and their nexus to transnational organized crime it is logical for the command to consider altering where to focus engagement. AFRICOM should maintain pressure in the East, but potentially could more effectively utilize its available means to accomplish ends through synergy and precedence on Africa's Oil Coast.

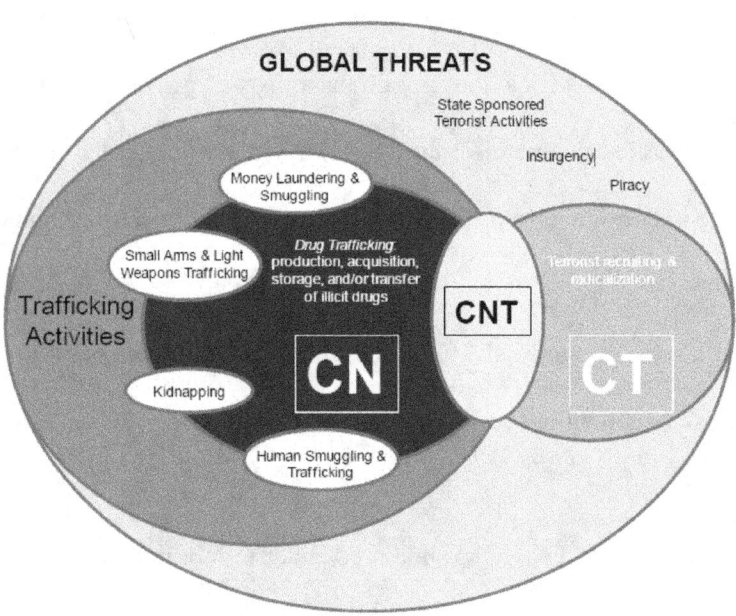

Figure 6. Interdependence of Illicit Trafficking and Violent Extremism
Source: Department of Defense. *Counternarcotics and Global Threats Strategy*. Washington,DC: Government Printing Office, 2011.

The synergistic effects of violent extremism and drug trafficking also threaten the region's vast oil resources. In 2012, Africa produced continent yields between eleven and twelve percent of the world's oil production.[64] Of that percentage, seven out of the world's top fifty oil producers reside on Africa's Oil Coast.[65] These nations surrounding the Gulf of Guinea are very important as they contain the majority of the continent's oil resources. In addition, the region is home to Nigeria and Angola, which are Africa's top two oil producers. Furthermore, five out of Africa's top ten oil producing nations are located within the Oil Coast, making the area vital as it holds Africa's largest concentration of crude oil resources.[66]

Nigeria is the largest oil producer in Africa, a member of the Organization of the Petroleum Exporting Countries (OPEC), holds the largest natural gas reserves on the continent, and is the world's fourth leading exporter of liquefied natural gas (LNG).[67] Nigeria's oil and natural gas resources are the mainstay of the country's economy. By far, the largest regional importer of Nigerian oil is Europe, importing forty four percent of the total in 2012. In 2012, the United States imported 406,000 barrels per day of crude oil from Nigeria, accounting for eighteen percent of Nigeria's total exports.[68] Nigeria is an important oil supplier to the United States, but the absolute volume and the share of U.S. imports from Nigeria has recently fallen. However, Nigeria has made up decreasing U.S. oil imports by rapidly expanding its market throughout Europe. In 2012, Nigerian oil exports to European countries rose by over forty percent.[69]

---

[64]Carolyn Gay, Department of Energy Advisor to US AFRICOM, interviewed by author, Fort Leavenworth, Kansas, 17 December 2013.

[65]U.S. Energy Information Administration, *Top World Oil Producers*, 2012, 1, http://www.eia.gov/countries/index.cfm/ (accessed 3 January 2014).

[66]Sammy Said, "Top 10 Oil Producing Countries in Africa, 2013," *The Richest* (24 April 2013): 1, http://www.therichest.com/expensive-lifestyle/location/top-10-oil-producing-countries-in-africa-2013/ (accessed 3 January 2014).

[67]U.S. Energy Information Association, *Nigeria Country Analysis Brief*, 30 December 2013, 1, http://www.eia.gov/countries/country-data.cfm?fips=NI/ (accessed 3 January 2014).

[68]Ibid., 12.

[69]Ibid., 13.

Even though the United States is not importing as much oil from Nigeria, Nigerian oil remains important to international markets, in which the U.S. is tied. As the United States and other partner nations strive to improve the structure of the international system, oil remains a critical component. Nigeria and other oil producing countries in the Gulf of Guinea are very important to the global market. The status of global supply and demand can affect crude oil prices.[70] Additionally, in his 2012 African Strategy President Obama highlights that by strengthening democratic organizations and boosting broad-based economic growth, Africa will reach its full potential in turn, generating greater prosperity and stability.[71] Thus, with oil as the lifeblood for most West African nations it is vital to building credible governance and economic institutions throughout the continent. Stable African institutions will improve global governance, commerce, and the world's economy.

In addition to Nigeria, the Gulf of Guinea is home to several other lucrative oil states. Angola is the continent's second leading oil producer and is rapidly growing in foreign investment. The country has substantial oil reserves and in 2012 produced almost two million barrels per day.[72] Angola's primary exports flow to China followed by the United States and Europe. Also Ghana has recently found success through offshore oil drilling and the establishment of deep water fields. Countries such as Equatorial Guinea, Congo-Brazzaville, Gabon, and Ghana contribute to the global oil market with Congo-Brazzaville and Ghana's production expected to increase.[73] Furthermore, the growing importance of oil throughout the

---

[70]Gay, interview.

[71]President Barack Obama, *U.S. Strategy for Africa*, 14 June 2012, 1, http://www.whitehouse.gov/the-press-office/2012/06/14/fact-sheet-new-strategy-toward-sub saharan-africa/ (accessed 3 January 2014).

[72]U.S. Energy Information Association, *Angola Country Analysis Brief*, 30 December 2013, http://www.eia.gov/countries/country-data.cfm?fips=AO/ (accessed 3 January 2014)

[73]Gay, interview.

region also is significant for the structural improvement of the Economic Community of West African States (ECOWAS).

ECOWAS aims to promote co-operation and integration in economic, social and cultural activity, ultimately leading to the establishment of an economic and monetary union through the total integration of the national economies of member states. It also aims to raise the living standards of its peoples, maintain and enhance economic stability, foster relations among member states and contribute to the progress and development of the African Continent.[74] Thus, to establish ECOWAS as a long-term credible institution, the United States and AFRICOM should consider prioritizing efforts on the Oil Coast. Through focused engagement and capacity building on the Oil Coast, violent extremism and illicit trafficking can be deterred ultimately facilitating regional stability. Furthermore, the creation of prosperous integrated oil economies will serve as a model for the entire African continent and provide significant benefits throughout the international system.

In summation, as highlighted in Figure 7, Africa's Oil Coast poses several interdependent threats that are very important to long-term American national interests and global security. The region should be a primary concern for senior U.S. policymakers and AFRICOM officials regarding the direction of African Foreign Policy. The spread of AQIM's presence from North Africa into Mali, Niger, and the uncontested Sahel region present formidable threats to continental security. AQIM's establishment of basing and recruitment sites in these areas could undermine long-term regional stability efforts. Similarly, the Nigerian based organization Boko Haram is expanding the size, lethality and scope of its terrorist operations. Furthermore, the growing partnership between AQIM and Boko Haram are of significant concern. Their abilities to

---

[74]African Union, *Profile: Economic Community of West African States (ECOWAS)*, 1-2, http://www.africa-union.org/root/au/recs/ECOWASProfile.pdf/ (accessed 3 January 2014).

consolidate finances, share safe havens, and mutually train to coordinate synchronized attacks portray significant challenges for international security.

The nexus for violent extremism is drug trafficking and transnational crime. Currently, Africa's Oil Coast is the hub of the world's drug trade. Weak governmental and security institutions, coupled with porous borders make the Oil Coast and Sahel region prominent locations for drug trafficking. Roughly fifty tons a year of cocaine from South America flows through the Oil Coast to the United States and Europe. The combination of violent extremism and illicit trafficking is undermining U.S. and international efforts throughout the region. Democratic reform and economic prosperity are being threatened posing significant challenges throughout the international system. The aforementioned hazards also endanger the region's vast oil production which remains important to the international economy and markets.

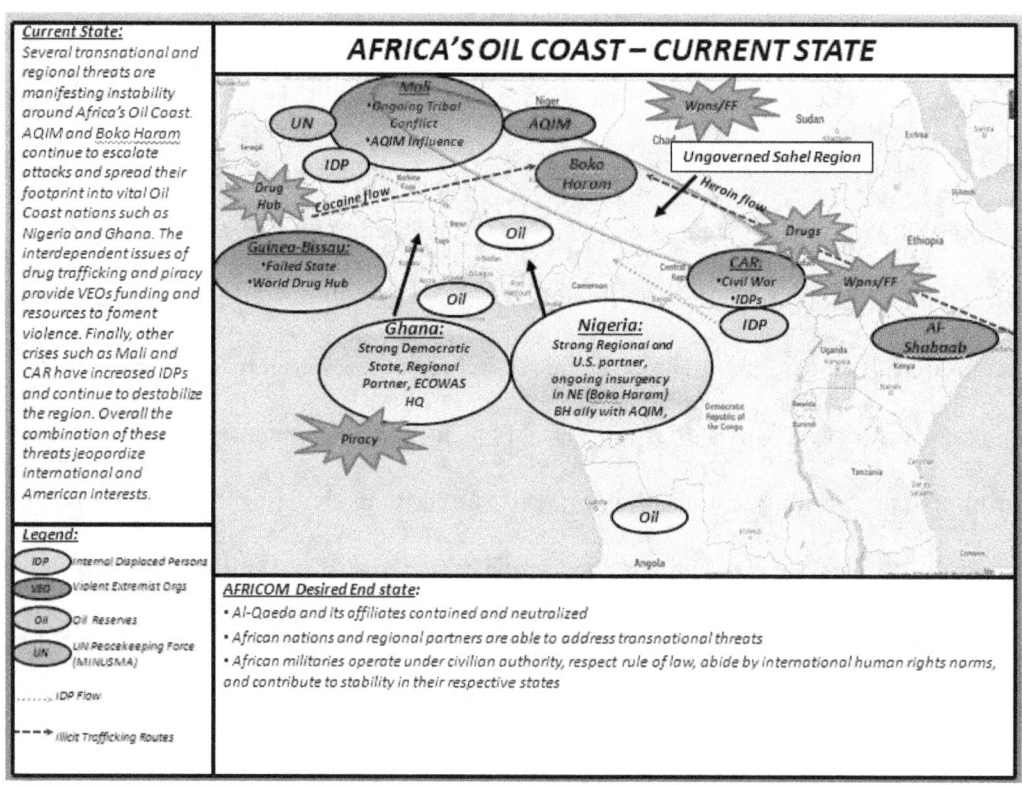

Figure 7. Africa's Oil Coast's Current State
Source: Created by author.

Considering the other ongoing issues throughout the African continent such as Al-Shabaab's operations and other crises in the East, coupled with the Arab Spring movements in the North, the U.S. is at a key crossroads regarding the trajectory of its African policy. Analyzing President Obama's 2012 African Strategy and AFRICOM Commander General David Rodriguez' recent mission statement and intent, a majority of their key tasks to facilitate strategic ends encompass Africa's Oil Coast. AFRICOM cannot be everywhere on the continent and must choose where to prioritize its efforts to maximize organizational effectiveness. Senior U.S. decision makers should consider providing AFRICOM with more resources or the combatant command and DOS should re-examine its current operational approach to focus more assets throughout the Oil Coast. By maintaining status quo in the East, and making the Oil Coast the continent's decisive operation the command can most effectively align its resources linking tactical actions to strategic ends across time and space. The researcher's assumption is that the proposed long-term strategy will facilitate better attainment of U.S. and international interests through the strengthening of democratic, economic, and regional security institutions which can create an arc of stability around the Gulf of Guinea and bolster a positive model for the entire continent.

AFRICOM CASE STUDY

This case study used George and Bennett's structured, focused approach to examine AFRICOM's current organizational structure and ability to interact throughout its external environment. This research paper concerns itself with one case study, broken into four sub-sections. The sub-sections primarily focus on examining the author's research questions presented in Chapter 1 of this study. The first section is an introduction and overview highlighting the evolution of AFRICOM as a combatant command. The second section examines the command's organizational design and capabilities to deter emerging threats throughout the continent, specifically on Africa's Oil Coast. The third section explores the command's assigned forces and allocated resources in order to facilitate linkage of tactical actions with strategic ends throughout its area of operations. The fourth section analyzes AFRICOM's effectiveness and aptitude to accomplish its key tasks and desired end state.

Overview

In the late 1990s and early 2000s, the United States began to recognize the growing geo-strategic importance of the African continent and its significance regarding American interests. The ability for organizations such as Al-Qaeda and other extremist organizations to build safe havens and foment violence triggered a monumental concern.[75] In addition, the region's rise in economic prosperity and abundance of natural resources fostered global attention. Similarly, the interdependent issues of poverty, poor governance, and economic inequality highlighted several problem sets that had the potential to manifest large scale instability throughout the continent and global environment.

Therefore, in 2007 President George W. Bush announced the creation of a new unified military command for the African continent with its own headquarters and staff.[76] AFRICOM marked a paradigm shift for U.S. combatant commands as its primary mission was not to fight wars but to develop and build partnerships through a whole of government approach. The command's design focused on leveraging U.S. soft power and the various instruments of national power, specifically diplomacy to help Africans solve African problems.[77] AFRICOM's organizational structure is non-traditional and novel in the fact that it is tasked to oversee

---

[75] Andre Le Sage, "Non-State Security Threats in Africa: Challenges for U.S. Engagement" *PRISM Magazine,* 2, no. 1 (December 2010): 59-61.

[76] Brown, 7.

[77] Ham, 2013 AFRICOM Posture Statement, 1.

traditional military activities and interagency programs that are funded through the State Department budget.[78]

Therefore, since 2007 the command has faced numerous challenges. First, the command does not have any assigned forces and receives allocation to execute theater objectives through the Global Force Management Implementation Guidance (GFMIG).[79] As witnessed from the Benghazi incident, this constraint makes it difficult to respond in times of crises In addition, AFRICOM has faced several difficulties earning the trust of African governments and their people. The command's headquarters is located in Germany, which is not on the continent and presents operational difficulties considering the enormous size of its area of operations.[80] Finally, the continuous interaction with interagency entities and achieving unity of effort to layer effects is a complex and daunting task.

However, given all the aforementioned challenges AFRICOM has continuously improved its ability to interact throughout its area of operations. The command has found creative ways to do more with less and leverage the JIIM environment for quality outputs. Through cross-functional integration of key interagency representatives across its staff, and collaborative venues to synchronize continental activities the command has made considerable progress and established a foothold in African affairs. Furthermore, through liaison officers at key institutions such as the African Union and ECOWAS, AFRICOM is starting to earn the trust of Africans.[81] In addition, continuous small-scale security cooperation exercises with finite resources are yielding positive effects.

---

[78]Volman, 37.

[79]CPT David Kemp, Chief of Human Resources Division at US AFRICOM, interviewed by author, Fort Leavenworth, Kansas, 17 December 2013.

[80]Isaac Kfir, "The Challenge that is US AFRICOM," *Joint Forces Quarterly*, 49, (2nd Quarter 2008): 112, http://www.ndupress.ndu.edu/ (accessed 1 October 2013).

[81]Kemp, interview.

Although the command has begun to generate quality outputs, the complexity and amalgamation of current problem sets throughout the continent poses several challenges that the organization may not be equipped or structured to negotiate. As the previous sections highlighted, the continent of Africa is facing many interdependent issues that have global implications. Senior decision makers should consider re-framing AFRICOM's current operational environment and the command's ability to accomplish its directed mission set. The researcher's working hypothesis for the study is that AFRICOM lacks a sufficient organizational structure to effectively build African capacity, deter threats, and protect American interests throughout the continent, specifically on its Oil Coast. The following sections of this case study will seek to provide further insights regarding the highlighted topic.

AFRICOM's Organizational Structure

Does AFRICOM have a sufficient organizational structure and capabilities to deter emerging threats throughout the continent, specifically on Africa's Oil Coast? Currently, AFRICOM is considered a combatant command plus. Upon its formation, the organization was given all the roles and responsibilities of a traditional combatant command but also a broader soft power mandate and larger contingent of personnel from other government agencies.[82] This different type of organizational structure was an anomaly across the joint force and illustrated the potential evolution of a combatant command.[83] The new organizational architecture sought to

---

[82]Lauren Ploch, "Africa Command: U.S. Strategic Interests and the Role of the U.S. Military in Africa," *Congressional Research Service,* (22 July 2011): 8, www.crs.gov/ (accessed 17 January 2014).

[83]Thomas S. Kuhn, *The Structure of Scientific Revolutions* (Chicago: University of Chicago Press, 1970), 1-9

facilitate a whole of government approach and better synchronize U.S. strategic efforts through unified action.[84]

AFRICOM consists of a headquarters and six subordinate commands. The headquarters staff has approximately 2,000 assigned personnel, including military, U.S. federal civilian employees, and U.S. contractor employees. Roughly 1,500 work at the command's headquarters in Stuttgart, Germany while others are assigned to AFRICOM units in Florida and England.[85] The organization's subordinate service component commands include U.S. Army Africa (USARAF), U.S. Naval Forces Africa (NAVAF), U.S. Marine Corps Forces Africa (MARFORAF), U.S. Air Forces Africa (AFAFRICA), U.S. Special Operations Command Africa (SOCAFRICA), and the Combined Joint Task Force-Horn of Africa (CJTF-HOA). The staff at the AFRICOM headquarters and majority of service component commands is located throughout the European continent. The exception is CJTF-HOA, AFRICOM's only operating base on the African continent established at Camp Lemonnier, Djibouti. AFRICOM's headquarters and subordinate organizations' structural configurations are very similar to Mary Jo Hatch's multi-divisional design template whereas staff sections are grouped by geographic regions or similarities in purpose and processes.[86] In military terminology the headquarters is a functional design, while the subordinate entities are arrayed by service component for interaction throughout the command's area of operations.[87]

---

[84]Department of Defense, Joint Publication (JP) 3-0, *Joint Operations* (Washington, DC: Government Printing Office, 2011), xi.

[85]U.S. African Command, *About the Command*, http://www.africom.mil/about-the-command/ (accessed 17 January 2014).

[86]Hatch and Cunliffe, 299.

[87]Department of Defense, JP 3-0, iv-8.

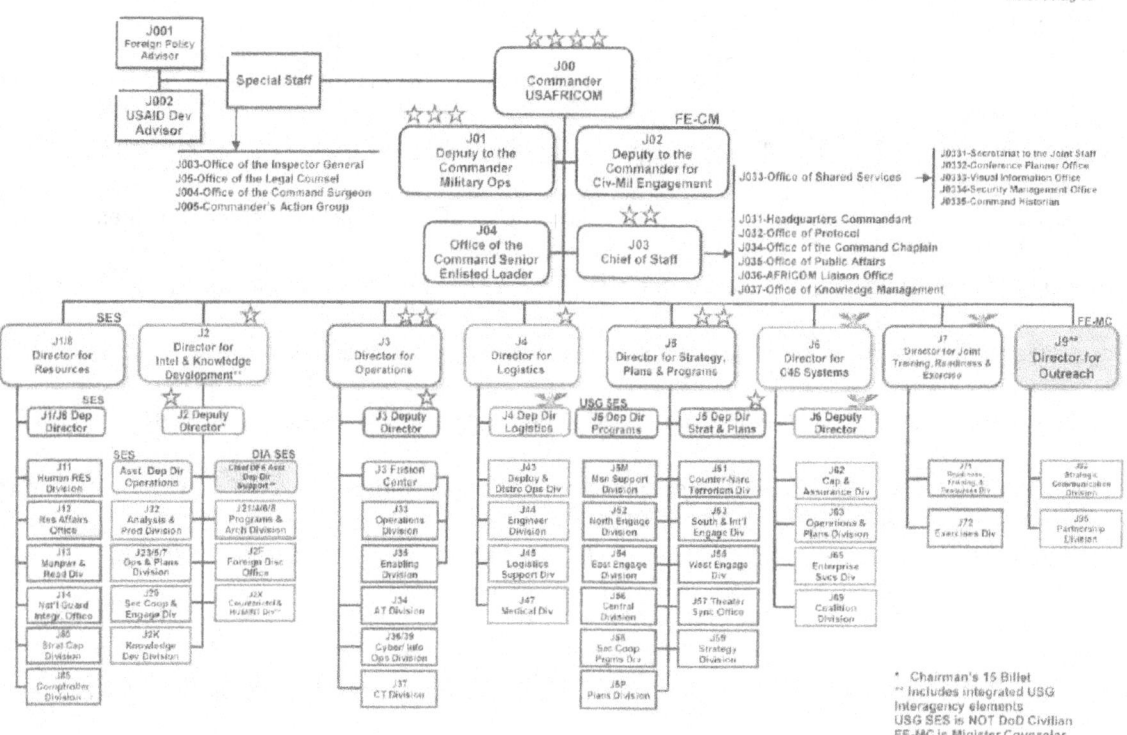

Figure 8. Headquarters Structural Design
Source: U.S. Africa Command, http://www.africom.mil/about-the-command

As highlighted in Figure 8, AFRICOM's headquarters staff is comprised of many joint

staff directorates that help the AFRICOM commander synchronize and direct joint operations.[88]

The command's functional design has yielded positive effects. First, the organization has

integrated interagency partners from the DOS and other governmental entities throughout several

joint functions. Currently, AFRICOM has thirty interagency members from eight different

agencies embedded across the staff.[89] In addition, the command has appointed a DOS Foreign

---

[88]Department of Defense, Joint Publication (JP) 3-33, *Joint Task Force Headquarters* (Washington, DC: Government Printing Office, 2012), xiv-xv.

[89]Kemp, interview.

Service Officer (FSO) as the Deputy to the Commander for Civil-Military Activities.[90] The command's whole of government approach has been a step in the right direction to improve coordination through unified action. However, as AFRICOM's operational environment continues to increase in complexity and threaten global security the organization may need to adapt its existing organizational structure to achieve desired effects.

Organizational theorists Paul Lawrence and Jay Lorsch argue that an organization's structure should reflect the conditions it faces in the environment.[91] The patterns and events occurring across the external sectors are constantly changing and significantly influence the organization. Therefore, it is necessary for an organization to understand the different characteristics of its environment in order to function effectively and adapt to different levels of uncertainty. In addition, theorist Richard Daft posits that an organization can adapt to its environment in numerous ways. As an open system, he states that the first area an organization should assess in a complex environment is its number and quality of inputs to meet desired outputs.[92]

In accordance with organizational theory, AFRICOM is a critical crossroads regarding the trajectory of its design and structure. The command has performed adequately with minimal assets and finite resources; however, due to the continents rapidly changing operational environment the organization is most likely not structured properly to accomplish its desired end state. The amalgamation of problem sets in the East and North coupled with emerging issues on the Oil Coast present AFRICOM with significant structural challenges. To effectively interact throughout its operational environment and build African capacity, AFRICOM should examine its number and type of inputs to achieve intended results. Assessment of the organization's size,

---

[90]Brown, 27.

[91]Lawrence and Lorsch, 8-13.

[92]Daft, 140-147.

specialization, and personnel ratios to complete designated functions may reveal potential shortfalls.[93]

Upon analysis of the current operational environment the researcher hypothesizes that a potential structural shortfall for AFRICOM is their number of interagency personnel. Originally, DOD officials testified that for AFRICOM to accomplish its broader soft power mandate and to better facilitate unified action, the command's overall staff should be comprised of twenty five percent interagency personnel.[94] Currently, AFRICOM's staff of 2000 assigned personnel consists of thirty interagency representatives. This enormous disparity falls significantly short in regards to U.S. DOD officials' initial intent and presents several questions in regards to the command's ability to synchronize and integrate with other governmental agencies for unity of effort.

AFRICOM's staff currently has the most interagency representatives of any combatant command; however, given the organization's unique mission set current DOD to interagency personnel ratios require re-assessment. The command was initially designed to showcase the evolution of a combatant command and provide a more balanced whole of government approach to capacity building on the African continent. However, the aforementioned ratios highlight that AFRICOM is far from balanced. AFRICOM's distinctive structure is not intended to militarize the region, but to facilitate unified action while integrating the instruments of national power to help Africans solve African problems. Due to AFRICOM's inadequate personnel ratios, the organization has encountered several challenges since its formation in 2007. One persistent theme is unity of effort between military and interagency personnel to synchronize engagement activities. AFRICOM has attempted to bridge this gap through the appointment of a DOS FSO as

---

[93]Ibid.
[94]Brown, 22.

the Deputy to the Commander for Civil-Military Activities.[95] The Deputy to the Commander for Civil-Military Activities serves as the primary integrator of interagency personnel assigned to the AFRICOM staff and is the organizations direct link to governmental agencies on the continent. In addition, AFRICOM has implemented creative solutions in an attempt to achieve better whole of government synchronization. The command has adapted its planning cycle by incorporating bi-annual conferences to foster collaboration regarding country and regional level objectives with African Chiefs of Mission and Host Nation Officials.[96] Furthermore, the DOS Deputy Commander has embedded interagency personnel across the AFRICOM staff's joint directorates to maximize productivity and cross functionality. Finally, the command created a fusion cell in the J-3 directorate to help facilitate better collaboration amongst the headquarters staff, African embassies, and U.S. based governmental agencies.[97]

The aforementioned techniques have worked satisfactorily; however, as African Affairs continue to escalate the command may require additional interagency representation to facilitate unified action. Currently, as violent extremism, civil wars, drug trafficking, piracy, and humanitarian issues increase across the continent and threaten U.S. interests, it is questionable if thirty interagency representatives can effectively help the command achieve African unity of effort. The DOS and several other governmental agencies currently are executing an abundance of initiatives throughout the area of operations. Ensuring synchronization of individual country plans and regional approaches to maximize the effects between AFRICOM and interagency personnel is critical. A battalion commander currently serving in the U.S. Army's 2nd Armored Brigade Combat Team, 1st Infantry Division (2/1 ABCT) regionally aligned to Africa recently highlighted some potential challenges he observed while deployed. He noted that military and

---

[95]Ibid., 27.

[96]Ibid., 51-52.

[97]Kemp, interview.

interagency personnel throughout Africa are making strides and improving relationships. However, that the achievement of unified effort is difficult primarily because many DOS country representatives and embassy teams have strategies that do not align.[98]

The divergent DOS country team strategies could present significant operational challenges for AFRICOM. The lack of a long-term whole of government plan of action for regional and continental capacity building efforts fails to maximize U.S. resources. AFRICOM's bi-annual conferences have improved this disconnect however issues remain. The resolution of this problem set is critical for helping Africans achieve long-term prosperity. As the crises in Mali, South Sudan, the Central African Republic (CAR), and Libya continue to manifest instability, improved DOD and DOS coordination is pivotal for conflict resolution. Specifically, on Africa's Oil Coast the emerging struggles in Mali and CAR will require more interagency personnel and closer coordination with AFRICOM to yield sustainable effects. If unity of effort is a problem now, it is only going to deteriorate. Holistically, the command's ability to synchronize ongoing and future interagency activities across the continent is questionable. Therefore, AFRICOM should consider altering its current organizational structure in order to identify viable options which increase the headquarters number of interagency personnel. This may assist in providing a more balanced and unified approach to African Affairs.

Another potential structural shortfall for AFRICOM is its civil-military operations (CMO) and civil affairs (CA) capabilities. AFRICOM's population centric mission focused on capacity building and a whole of government approach requires extensive information regarding the civil domain for decision-making. According to Joint Publication (JP) 3-57 CMO and CA staff representatives establish, maintain, influence, or exploit relationships between U.S. military forces, indigenous forces, and host nation institutions. Furthermore, they provide running

---

[98]LTC John Mountford, Commander for 1-7 Field Artillery Battalion, interviewed by author, Fort Leavenworth, Kansas, 24 January 2014.

assessments in regards to areas, structures, organizations, populations, and environment throughout the area of operations.[99]

A documented problem throughout AFRICOM headquarters is the organization's ability to acquire civil domain information from subordinate units and other interagency entities for future planning.[100] Furthermore, the staff at AFRICOM's headquarters does not have the right amount of specialization to properly analyze and integrate civil information. This is a monumental structural shortfall as the command's primary strategy centers on civil engagement to yield non-kinetic effects.[101] Continuous civil information assessments throughout African nations are a critical requirement for AFRICOM to accomplish its intended purpose. Lieutenant Colonel (LTC) John Mountford, a battalion commander with 2/1 ABCT's regionally aligned forces (RAF) confirmed this structural shortfall from his recent operations in the Oil Coast's country of Guinea. Overall, prior to his organization's security cooperation mission the unit was provided very minimal information regarding the threat of his future area of operations due to lack of reporting and civil information.[102] Also, throughout execution a central point for all members of the JIIM environment to collect, synthesize, and share civil information was non-existent. This structural deficiency is a substantial concern as it highlights a lack of unity of effort placing American lives at undue risk. Furthermore, AFRICOM and JIIM partners are missing vital opportunities to learn about the cultures of various African nations for the construction of effective narratives to inform and influence the regions populous. Therefore, the researcher

---

[99]Department of Defense, Joint Publication (JP) 3-57, *Civil-Military Operations* (Washington, DC: Government Printing Office 2013), I-1-5.

[100]Sharon Anderson, "Improving Civil Affairs Planning in the African AOR," *CHIPS: The Department of Navy's Information Technology Magazine*, (July 2012): 1, http://www.doncio.navy.mil/ CHIPS/ArticleDetails.aspx?id=4048/ (accessed 23 January 2014).

[101]Ibid.

[102]Mountford, interview.

hypothesizes that AFRICOM requires these critical capabilities to mitigate risk and facilitate the commander's understanding and visualization of his operational environment.

In conjunction with the researcher's previously highlighted structural shortfalls, AFRICOM also faces the difficult task of cutting its headquarters by twenty percent. Secretary of Defense (SECDEF) Chuck Hagel's recently announced initiative to cut combatant commands' staff by twenty percent poses significant challenges for AFRICOM as it is already lacking sufficient personnel ratios and specialization.[103] Due to the SECDEF's directive, the continent's increasing volatility, and emergence of threats on its Oil Coast AFRICOM faces difficult decisions about its organizational configuration and design. The command must develop creative and innovative solutions, which maximize organizational effectiveness throughout its operational environment. AFRICOM should assess its current joint directorates for identification of redundancies that can be truncated and streamlined via reach back to U.S. based organizations. A potential example is the command's J-2 intelligence directorate that is composed of several hundred personnel spread across the organization's multiple headquarters locations. AFRICOM could decrease its intelligence staff while still maintaining current capabilities by leveraging U.S. based Defense Intelligence Agency (DIA) and DOS Bureau of Intelligence and Research existing assets.[104] Examining each directorate in this manner could help meet the SECDEF's guidance while simultaneously increasing specialized interagency and civil military personnel.

Additionally, through an upgraded network structure AFRICOM could find ways to meet the SECDEF's guidance while improving specialized personnel ratios. Organizational theorist Mary Jo Hatch highlights the benefits of investing and building a robust network structure. She

---

[103]Marcus Weisberger, "DoD Begins Cutting Staff Sizes, Will Reorganize Policy Office," *Defense News*, (5 December 2013): 1, http://www.defensenews.com/article/20131205/ DEFREG02/312050012/DoD-Begins-Cutting-Staff-Sizes-Will-Reorganize-Policy-Office/ (accessed 28 January 2014).

[104]Brown, 86-88.

posits that advances in information technology and the network are enabling organizations to become smaller while increasing outputs and information flow throughout their environment.[105] In accordance with Mary Jo Hatch, AFRICOM should consider establishing a network that facilitates shared understanding across the entire JIIM environment. Due to the increasing complexity of the African system combined with AFRICOM's minimal resources and headquarters location the organization needs to find innovative ways to execute mission command. The command's creation of a single technological medium that connects subordinate components, interagency personnel, intergovernmental entities, and key multinational and African institutions is critical. Ultimately, through maximizing network capabilities AFRICOM can effectively exercise mission command through the creation of collaborative venues improving unity of effort and building cohesive teams through mutual trust.[106]

AFRICOM's Forces and Allocated Resources

Does AFRICOM have sufficient forces and allocated resources to facilitate linkage of tactical actions with strategic ends throughout its area of operations? Since AFRICOM's establishment, the command has continuously reacted to its dynamic operational environment. Due to the organization's unique structure and mission set, the command has encountered several challenges to maintaining a position of relative advantage throughout the African continent. Specifically, assignment of forces and allocation of resources are obstacles hindering AFRICOM's ability to interact throughout its area of operations.

---

[105]Hatch and Cunliffe, 307.

[106]Department of the Army, Army Doctrinal Reference Publication (ADRP) 3-0, *United Land Operations* (Washington, DC: Government Printing Office, 2012), 2-10-2-11.

Since AFRICOM's initial formation in 2008, the command has not been assigned forces.[107] Furthermore, due to ongoing wars in Iraq and Afghanistan the organization was not a priority for resourcing. Additionally, senior U.S. leaders were sensitive to African cultural perceptions and did not want to illustrate American militarization on the continent.[108] The United States wanted to help Africans solve African problems through their own assets and solutions. AFRICOM has done an exceptional job doing more with less; however, as the continent is on the edge of chaos the researcher hypothesizes that the command should attain higher strategic priority and requires increased resourcing for mission accomplishment.

After the Benghazi incident, senior U.S. leaders began recognizing the strategic magnitude associated with Africa.[109] Correspondingly, U.S. officials have incrementally increased AFRICOM's force allocation to accomplish theater specific objectives and protect vital U.S. interests. In 2011, a Special Purpose Marine Air Ground Task Force (SP-MAGTF) comprised of roughly 200 personnel was charged with supporting AFRICOM's theater security cooperation requirements. The SP-MAGTF is a scalable and tailorable force package that conducts military training, provides limited crisis response capability, civil-military operations personnel and foreign humanitarian assistance.[110] The SP-MAGTF conducts combatant commander directed mission sets throughout Africa.[111] The SP-MAGTF has yielded positive effects and remains a critical component of AFRICOM.

---

[107]Kemp, interview.

[108]Keenan, 18-20.

[109]Chivvis and Liepman, 7-8.

[110]David L. Morgan, "A SPMAGTF is a key element for securing strategic access and partnership with African nations," *Marine Corps Gazette*, (December 2012): 1, http://www.mca-marines.org/gazette/article/marine-forces-africa/ (accessed 27 January 2014).

In addition, the U.S. Army announced its RAF construct in 2012. This initiative provided combatant commanders' with aligned forces for theater specific objectives. AFRICOM was the first organization to receive forces as a part of the U.S. Army's new theory of action. In 2012 the 2/1 ABCT and eight National Guard battalions were formally aligned with AFRICOM to conduct military-to-military engagements, participate in exercises or train units preparing to serve as peacekeepers.[112] In 2013, the RAF conducted over 100 small scale engagements throughout the African continent while simultaneously providing force protection and limited crisis response for CJTF-HOA at Camp Lemonnier, Djibouti.[113] The SP-MAGTF and RAF have significantly helped willing African nations develop internal capacity while building important relationships. However, as the continent continues to escalate in volatility the command may require more forces to assist African nations in bolstering internal security and governance.

The alignment of the SP-MAGTF and RAF have provided AFRICOM with additional capability, however the continent's increasing complexity necessitates more assets. Organizational theorist Richard Daft highlights that an organization is successful when it brings together resources to achieve desired goals and outcomes.[114] Furthermore, through constant assessment of the external environment organizations continuously modify inputs seeking innovative ways to sustain a competitive advantage and distribute services more efficiently. Inputs to an organizational system include employees, money, information, and other physical

---

[111]Ed Galo, "Lejeune Marines start new rotation of Special-Purpose Marine Air-Ground Task Force Africa," *Jacksonville News*, 27 January 2014, http://www.jdnews.com/jdnewstream/lejeune-marines-start-new-rotation-of-special-purpose-marine-air-ground-task-force-africa-read-more-1.268405/ (accessed 27 January 2014).

[112]Michele Tan, "AFRICOM: Regionally Aligned Forces Find Their Anti-terror Mission," *Defense News*, (20 October 2013): 1, http://www.defensenews.com/article/20131020/SHOWSCOUT04/310200014/ (accessed 27 January 2014).

[113]Ibid.

[114]Daft, 13.

resources.[115] Analyzing the African system, even with the addition of the SP-MAGTF and the RAF conflicts have continued to intensify. Several African nations still require additional military, security, and governmental assistance to deter threats. The United States and AFRICOM cannot fix the continent's problems on its own, but it can more effectively accomplish its soft power mandate through additional resourcing. Specifically, on Africa's Oil Coast capacity building and host nation military training is critical. Currently, the region is at a monumental point in time whereas the trajectory of transnational threats can be defeated or amplify largely dependent on increased U.S. assistance. Numerous Oil Coast countries such as Guinea, Ghana, and Nigeria have displayed willingness to counter transnational threats and improve governmental affairs but require additional training and means.[116] Currently, AFRICOM is doing the best it can to build capacity throughout the continent however it does not possess the right amount of inputs to achieve desired outputs.

From a force prospective, a good scenario to examine is AFRICOM's recent participation in the ongoing South Sudan crisis. In the midst of South Sudan's civil war numerous American and western diplomats in Juba required evacuation.[117] AFRICOM utilized Special Operations Forces and a platoon from CJTF-HOA's response force to facilitate recovery of non-combatant personnel. During the evacuation attempt, several aircraft received small-arms fire and four U.S. servicemen were injured.[118] Therefore, the command employed the SP-MAGTF for follow on assistance. Roughly three days after the initial evacuation attempt, 150 Marines arrived to support

---

[115]Ibid., 12.

[116]Mountford, interview.

[117]Eyder Peralta, "Four U.S. Service Members Injured In South Sudan," *NPR*, (21 December 2013): 1, http://www.npr.org/blogs/thetwo-way/2013/12/21/256007086/four-u-s-service-members-injured-in-south-sudan/ (accessed 27 January 2014).

[118]Ibid.

the mission.[119] Eventually, designated civilian personnel were evacuated and the operation resulted in success for AFRICOM.

However, AFRICOM and senior U.S. officials must not get overconfident and utilize the South Sudan crisis as a case study to illustrate how the command still lacks necessary forces. If a small non-combatant evacuation consumed almost all of AFRICOM's aligned forces, imagine the impacts when multiple crises occur simultaneously. Hypothetically, consider that several violent extremist organizations' such as Al-Shabaab, AQIM, and Boko Haram studied AFRICOM's recent response. Through the terrorist organizations growing collaboration and synergy they could collectively launch synchronized attacks across the continent yielding catastrophic effects. Al-Shabaab could incite a crisis in the east, while AQIM attacks western targets in the north, culminating with a Boko Haram attack on an American target in Nigeria. Considering even two out of the three occurred, the researcher hypothesizes that neither Host Nation forces, African Standby forces, or AFRICOM could effectively safeguard U.S. personnel and vital interests. The aforementioned scenario provides a small snapshot illustrating how the continent's growing complexity and emergence of transnational threats, specifically on Africa's Oil Coast, may cause operational challenges for AFRICOM as currently constructed.

In addition to adequate force allocation, AFRICOM also has significant resource constraints, which limit organizational effectiveness. One significant issue is theater sustainment. As the RAF and other forces conduct training exercises and security cooperation missions throughout the continent logistical support is paramount. Currently, AFRICOM does not have a dedicated theater sustainment command. The 21st Theater Sustainment Command's primary mission is to support the U.S. Army European Command (USAREUR) and as directed,

---

[119]John Vandiver, "South Sudan crisis lands Marine crisis response unit its largest mission," *Stars and Stripes*, 24 December 2013, http://www.stripes.com/news/south-sudan-crisis-lands-marine-crisis-response-unit-its-largest-mission-1.259075/ (accessed 27 January 2014).

AFRICOM.[120] This shortfall is another principal concern as it limits a primary element of operational art called operational reach. The vagaries of history have repeatedly illustrated the importance of logistical support in military operations. As Clausewitz notes, "military forces remain dependent on its sources of supply and replenishment as they constitute the basis of their existence and survival."[121] Recent operations by U.S. forces in Africa have encountered logistical shortfalls that are alarming. Units are relying on host nation assistance and embassy facilitation for critical requirements such as bottled water, communication support, and force protection. However, oftentimes these logistical necessities are difficult to coordinate and finding contract support is problematic.[122] Therefore, as U.S. military engagement efforts continue to increase throughout Africa this structural deficiency requires modification to maximize effectiveness.

AFRICOM's Organizational Effectiveness

Given the unique design of AFRICOM and its geographic challenges, is the organization effectively accomplishing its key tasks and desired end state throughout Africa, specifically its Oil Coast? Organizational theorist Amitai Etzioni defines organizational effectiveness as the "degree to which an organization achieves its goals" and as "a desired state of affairs which the organization attempts to realize."[123] In military terminology, units measure their effectiveness through continuous assessment of the operational environment. Assessment is a process that measures progress of the joint force toward mission accomplishment. Furthermore, it compares

---

[120]U.S. Army Europe Command, 21st Theater Sustainment Brigade, http://www.eur.army.mil/21TSC/mission.asp/ (accessed 29 January 2014).

[121]Carl von Clausewitz, *On War*, trans. Michael Howard and Peter Paret (Princeton University Press, 1989), 341.

[122]Mountford, interview.

[123]Etzioni, 6.

forecasted outcomes with actual events to determine overall effectiveness.[124] Organizational

theorists utilize four standard frameworks to assess organizational effectiveness known as the

goal-based approach, resource-based approach, internal process approach, and stakeholders

approach.[125] For this case study the researcher used the goal-based approach to examine

AFRICOM's current operational efficiency

The goal-based approach defines effectiveness in terms of outputs and how well an

organization accomplishes its goals.[126] Currently AFRICOM's key tasks are countering violent

extremist organizations, support defense institution building, strengthening maritime security,

supporting peace operations, supporting humanitarian and disaster response, and to counter illicit

trafficking. Furthermore, the organization's end state is that Al-Qaeda and its affiliates are

contained and neutralized, African states and institutions can counter transnational threats, and

assisting African states in building capable militaries to provide stability.[127]

Analyzing the commands effectiveness in countering violent extremism and containing

Al-Qaeda is interesting. Since AFRICOM's formation in 2007, Al-Qaeda has continued to pave

the way for several other extremist organizations to commence activities throughout Africa.

Furthermore, they have developed subordinate entities and established cooperative ties with

African Islamic militants to intensify extremist operations. Affiliates such as Al- Shabaab, AQIM,

and Boko Haram have increased actions and lethality. Specifically from 2007-2010 the rise of

terrorist attacks per year exponentially increased throughout Africa from roughly 300 incidents to

---

[124]Department of Defense, Joint Publication (JP) 5-0, *Joint Operation Planning*, (Washington, DC: Government Printing Office, 2011), D-1.

[125]Hodge, Anthony, and Gales, 75.

[126]Ibid.

[127]General David Rodriguez. AFRICOM's Mission and Commander's Intent, 29 July 2013, http://www.africom.mil (accessed 28 August 2013).

500.[128] In 2011, violent extremism continued to spike throughout the continent reaching its peak with over 978 attacks.[129] On Africa's Oil Coast, Boko Haram's trend of violence continued throughout 2012, escalating attacks killing roughly 770 people.[130] Furthermore, in 2013 the organizations operations have increased and spread outside Nigerian borders. Recent kidnappings of westerners in Mali and Cameroon illustrate the groups growing influence. In addition, reported collaboration and links with Al-Qaeda mark the potential for the organization to become a transnational threat.[131]

The significant increase in violent extremism and Al-Qaeda operations throughout Africa is very troubling and intriguing. Since 2007, the African system has exponentially grown in complexity. Correspondingly, from its inception AFRICOM has faced an uphill struggle adapting to its dynamic external environment. Considering the aforementioned challenges the command has operated effectively with minimal resources. AFRICOM and DOS initiatives such as the Trans-Sahara Counterterrorism Partnership (TSCTP) program aimed at defeating terrorist organizations by strengthening regional counterterrorism capabilities in the Pan-Sahel of Africa has been a step in the right direction.[132] Additionally, limited military engagement with some Oil Coast countries through the United Nations Multidimensional Integrated Stabilization Mission in

---

[128]Universityof Maryland, *Global Terrorism Database,* http://www.start.umd.edu/gtd (accessed 19 November 2013).

[129]United States Department of State, *National Counterterrorism Center: Country Reports on Terrorism 2011* (31 July 2012), http://www.state.gov/j/ct/rls/crt/2011/195555.htm (accessed 19 November 2013).

[130]Scott Stewart, *Is Boko Haram More Dangerous Than Ever,* (13 December 2012): 2-4, http://www.stratfor.com/weekly/boko-haram-more-dangerous-ever (accessed 23 November 2013).

[131]Ham, 2013 AFRICOM Posture Statement, 10.

[132]United States Africa Command, *Security Cooperation Programs,* http://www.africom.mil/what-we-do/security-cooperation-programs (accessed 26 November 2013).

Mali (MINUSMA) have yielded positive effects and improved African capacity to counter AQIM.[133]

Similarly, in the east AFRICOM's CJTF-HOA coupled with the African Union's mission in Somalia (AMISOM) are impacting Al-Shabaab's operational capabilities. However, the latest Al-Shabaab related attack on September 21, 2013 at the Nairobi Mall in Kenya, killing sixty-eight civilians illustrates that the extremist organization still poses a significant threat in the region.[134] Overall, the numbers highlighted above clearly demonstrate that Al-Qaeda and violent extremism remains major threats to Africa and the international system. Furthermore, African nations require additional military support to adequately deter threats and provide continental security. Thus, the researcher hypothesizes that AFRICOM has operated effectively with the means available. Conversely, from a theoretical goal-based approach, AFRICOM has not sufficiently contained or neutralized Al-Qaeda. The command has achieved an initial foothold and made significant strides but requires more resources to accomplish its end state.

Correspondingly, the interdependent and interrelated tasks of providing maritime security and countering illicit trafficking are very challenging. Over the last couple of years, AFRICOM has done a tremendous job in deterring piracy on the continents east coast. Through effective security cooperation programs such as the Africa Partnership Station and African Maritime Law Enforcement partnership, African states are starting to build capacity to deter piracy and drug trafficking. Specifically, from 2011-2012 attacks in the Gulf of Aden have decreased from 237 to seventy-five, illustrating AFRICOM's success.[135]

---

[133]Mountford, interview.

[134]Ishaan Tharoor, "Terror in Nairobi: Behind al-Shabab's War With Kenya," *Time* (23 September 2013): 1-2, http://world.time.com/2013/09/21/terror-in-nairobi-behind-al-shabaabs-war-with-kenya (accessed 19 November, 2013).

However, as piracy is declining in East Africa it is on the rise on the continent's Oil Coast. The production of three million barrels of oil per day, equaling about one third of Africa's output, located around the Gulf of Guinea has created a target rich environment for hijackers.[136] Piracy incidents recorded off Africa's West Coast rose from forty-nine in 2011 to fifty eight in 2012. Furthermore, the number of attacks in 2013 is currently double those in 2012.[137] Hence, even though the command has been effective in the east, piracy still poses significant threats to West African states. On Africa's Oil Coast, the money garnered from piracy related activities is furthering instability throughout the region. The direct investment of pirate finances into criminal activities, human trafficking, building militias, and supporting extremist organizations is greater than ever. Therefore, utilizing the goal-based approach methodology the researcher assesses that while AFRCIOM has yielded positive effects in the east, the command should consider placing more emphasis on building maritime capacity throughout Africa's Oil Coast.

In conjunction with violent extremism and piracy, drug trafficking has been a problem in Africa for many decades. Currently in East and South Africa, the heroin trade from Afghanistan remains prevalent. Furthermore, data from the 2013 United Nations Drug Report illustrates between 2010 and 2012 that heroin trafficking in Africa has increased over fivefold.[138] Similarly,

---

[135]International (ICC) Chamber of Commerce Commercial Crime Services, *Piracy Falls in 2012, but seas off East and West Africa Remain Dangerous* (London: ICC Commercial Crime Services, 2013), 1, http://www.icc-ccs.org/news/836-piracy-falls-in-2012-but-seas-off-east-and-west-africa-remain-dangerous-says-imb (accessed 25 November 2013).

[136]Faith Karimi, "African pirates use millions of dollars in ransom on drugs, real estate, prostitutes," *CNN*, (2 November 2013): 1, http://www.cnn.com/2013/11/02/world/africa/horn-of-africa-piracy-loot/ (accessed 25 November 2013).

[137]Meagan Clark, "Pirates Off West Africa's Coast Threatening African Oil, Focus Of Anti-Piracy Concerns Shifting From Horn Of Africa To West Africa," *IB Times*, (November 2013): 1, http://www.ibtimes.com/pirates-west-africas-coast-threatening-african-oil-focus-anti-piracy-concerns-shifting-horn-africa (accessed 25 November 2013).

[138]United Nations Office on Drugs and Crime, *World Drug Report 2013* (Vienna, Austria: United Nations 2013), 33.

on Africa's Oil Coast cocaine shipments from Colombia and South America have risen significantly. An estimated one third of exported Colombian cocaine or two hundred tons moves through Africa's Oil Coast.

Nevertheless, through effective security cooperation programs African states are starting to build capacity to counter illicit trafficking. AFRICOM has constructed a CN-LEA to focus more emphasis on drug trafficking. The CN-LEA's priority is Africa's Oil Coast. However, as Mark Huebschman the Deputy Chief, Counter Narcotics and Law Enforcement Division at AFRICOM highlights measuring effectiveness is difficult.[139] The continent takes two steps forward and one back due to corruption and lack of governance.[140] The CN-LEA has roughly a twenty million dollar annual budget for countering illicit trafficking. Also, AFRICOM has limited naval assets available to conduct maritime interdiction and security cooperation. The command does the best it can with limited means, but the assets and funding do not go far.[141] Through mobile training teams with SOCAFRICA, MARFORAF, and USARAF the organization has made a difference. Recently in Ghana, AFRICOM and Joint Interagency Task Force South (JIATF-S) coordinated with host nation forces to conduct a massive cocaine seizure.[142] These operations are rare but are excellent examples of what AFRICOM can accomplish. Using the goal-based approach the researcher assesses that AFRICOM's efforts countering illicit trafficking have been moderately effective. However, to truly yield long-term impacts and accomplish the desired end state the organization requires additional resourcing and DOS assistance for success.

Finally, AFRICOM has generated moderate effects throughout the continent building institutions, supporting peace operations and providing humanitarian assistance. The creation of

---

[139]Huebschman, interview.

[140]Ibid.

[141]Ibid.

[142]Ibid.

institutions such as ECOWAS, AMISOM and WACSI has helped Africans establish venues to solve African problems and build long term prosperity. However, due to the continents growing instability, corruption, and poor governance these associations are far from credible and will require extensive U.S. assistance for desired outputs. Similarly, through effective coordination with the African Union and U.N., AFRICOM has achieved positive results in humanitarian and peace operations. Programs such as the African Contingency and Training Assistance (ACOTA) and Counter Lord's Resistance Army (LRA) are helping to build African capacity for response to humanitarian conflicts and issues.[143] Nevertheless, current cycles of violence in the CAR, the Democratic Republic of Congo (DRoC), and South Sudan present enormous problems.[144] These pockets of violence are becoming breeding grounds for extremists and various armed groups. Furthermore, the issues could develop into religious and ethnic conflicts with long-standing consequences, and even civil wars that could spread into neighboring countries. Consequently, even though AFRICOM has generated moderate effects, it will require more inputs to achieve its desired end state in the anticipated operational environment.

CHAPTER V: CONCLUSION AND RECOMMENDATIONS

Conclusion

Due to Africa's current operational environment, AFRICOM is at a critical crossroads regarding the trajectory of its organizational design. Since the command's formation in 2007, AFRICOM has performed superbly with minimal assets and finite resources; however, due to the continent's dynamic operational environment the organization may require structural alteration to accomplish its directed mission and desired end state. The South Sudan crisis and Al-Shabaab's presence in the East coupled with the northern Arab Spring movement has drawn most of

---

[143]United States Africa Command. *Security Cooperation Programs.*

[144]BBC News, "Central African Republic descending into chaos," 26 November 2013, http://www.bbc.co.uk/news/world-africa-25095471 (accessed 26 November 2013).

AFRICOM's attention. However, the manifestation of several transnational threats on Africa's Oil Coast requires immediate attention. The Oil Coast is a significant region of vast strategic importance to the United States and international system. As the Oil Coast is on the brink of disaster, AFRICOM should re-assess its operational approach and organizational structure for linking tactical actions to strategic ends across time and space.

Currently, on Africa's Oil Coast violent extremism, illicit drug trafficking, and lucrative oil resources represent interdependent subjects that are manifesting instability. These emergent transnational threats are posing significant challenges to several countries in the region such as Nigeria, Ghana, Cameroon, and Guinea that are attempting to achieve long term prosperity. Specifically, violent extremism on the Oil Coast is becoming a major problem set. According to former AFRICOM commander, General Carter Ham, AQIM, which operates on the periphery of the Oil Coast in Northern Mali and the desolate Sahel region, is currently the most direct African concern to near-term U.S. national security interests.[145] As illustrated from the Benghazi attack in 2012 and the hostage incident at the Algerian In Amenas gas facility in 2013, AQIM remains a formidable threat.[146] The organization has the potential to continue terrorist attacks along the southern axis into the Sahel and to the north into the Iberian Peninsula. The instability and lack of security in broad swaths of northern Africa, large parts of the Sahel and Africa's Oil Coast offer AQIM rich opportunities to transit, recruit, raise funds, plot, and conduct operations.[147] Their activities could further de-stabilize Oil Coast governments, deter democratic reform, impede military development, and stifle economic growth.

Similarly, another extremist organization based in the Oil Coast country of Nigeria labeled Boko Haram poses major challenges. Boko Haram is a militant Islamist group fighting for

---

[145]Ham, 2013 AFRICOM Posture Statement, 8.

[146]Ibid.

[147]Ibid.

the implementation of Islamic law in Nigeria. Over the last few years the organization's operations have significantly increased in attacks and lethality. Boko Haram has upgraded its tactics from simple attacks to incite sectarian violence to sophisticated mass-casualty attacks incorporating suicide vests and vehicle borne improved explosive devices targeting civilians.[148]

The Nigerian Armed Forces coupled with training and support from the United States and international actors have initiated an attempt to defeat Boko Haram's movement. However from 2010 to the present day, the extremist organization has answered the counter-insurgency by increasing operations. Furthermore, Boko Haram has begun to expand its operations outside Nigerian borders. Recent kidnappings of westerners in Mali and Cameroon illustrate the groups growing influence. In December 2012, former AFRICOM Commander General Carter Ham compared Boko Haram's status to that of Al Qaeda in the 1990s and highlighted the group's strategic magnitude.[149] Furthermore, increased collaboration between AQIM and Boko Haram are of grave concern highlighting the growing potential for the organizations to merge and conduct international operations.[150]

In addition to violent extremism, piracy and drug trafficking are also fostering instability on Africa's Oil Coast. Over the last few years, the Oil Coast has emerged as a key player in the trafficking of drugs.[151] The attraction of the regions porous borders, corrupt law enforcement capacities, lack of interstate cooperation, and its ease of accessibility through unmonitored ports

---

[148]Stewart, 2.

[149]General Carter Ham, "Counterterrorism in Africa," speech at The Homeland Security Policy Institute, 3 December 2012, 10, http://www.gwumc.edu/hspi/events/ GENHamPRF416.cfm/ (accessed 22 January 2014).

[150]Ham, 2013 AFRICOM Posture Statement.

[151]Justine Lindeman, *Global Drug Trafficking: Africa's Expanding Role* (Washington DC: Woodrow Wilson International Center for Scholars, 2009), 6.

and airstrips has helped to make Africa's Oil Coast the world's hub of drug operations.[152] Congruently, as piracy is declining in East Africa it is on the rise on the continent's Oil Coast. The production of 3 million barrels of oil per day, equaling about one third of Africa's output, located around the Gulf of Guinea has created a target rich environment for hijackers.[153] Piracy incidents recorded off Africa's Oil Coast have more than doubled from 2011 to 2013. Holistically drug trafficking and piracy are significantly contributing to the spread of violent extremism throughout Africa and its Oil Coast. Terrorist organizations and non-state actors can use the region as a safe haven and economic base to fund activities. The availability of large sums of money allows extremists to purchase weapons, conduct operations, and potentially buy political power through less violent means.[154]

The synergistic effects of violent extremism, drug trafficking, and piracy also threaten the region's vast oil resources. In 2012, Africa produced between eleven to twelve percent of the total world oil production.[155] Of that percentage, seven out of the world's top fifty oil producers reside on Africa's Oil Coast.[156] In addition, the region is home to Nigeria and Angola, which are the continent's top two oil producers. Furthermore, five out of Africa's top ten oil-producing nations are located within the Oil Coast, making the area vital as it holds Africa's largest concentration of crude oil resources.[157]

Although in recent years the United States has decreased oil imports from the Gulf of Guinea, the commodity remains a vital interest. For Gulf of Guinea oil producing nations' oil is

---

[152]Ibid., 4.

[153]Karimi, 1.

[154]Ibid., 13.

[155]Gay, interview.

[156]U.S. Energy Information Administration, *Top World Oil Producers, 2012*, 1.

[157]Said, 1.

important to their domestic economies and to the global market.[158] In his 2012 African Strategy, President Obama highlights that by boosting broad-based economic growth, Africa will reach its full potential generating greater prosperity and stability.[159] Accordingly, with oil as the lifeblood for most Gulf of Guinea nations it is a primary ingredient for the construction of stable African institutions. Therefore, as the United States and other partner nations strive to improve the structure of the international system, African oil remains a critical component.

Overall, Africa's Oil Coast has manifested into an arc of instability that can directly threaten global security. President Obama's 2012 U.S. strategy for Africa specifies four mutually reinforcing pillars for continental success. By strengthening democratic institutions, spurring economic growth, advancing security, and promoting long-term development the United States can assist African's in their attainment of greater prosperity.[160] Furthermore, in his 2012 National Security Strategy President Obama highlights countering terrorism and the defeat of Al-Qaeda or its affiliates as the core concern of the United States.[161] Analyzing, the Presidents national strategy and African pillars it is clear that the Oil Coast should be a top priority because of the region's growing terrorist threat, democratic potential, and importance to the global economy. Since 2007, AFRICOM has done an exceptional job establishing a foothold on the continent and building African capacity; however, the emerging threats on the Oil Coast require more consideration for the command to achieve its desired end state. Therefore, the researcher hypothesizes that AFRICOM should consider adapting its operational approach to concentrate resources where it can most effectively layer them to protect U.S. interests.

---

[158]Gay, interview.

[159]President Barack Obama, "U.S. Strategy for Africa," 1.

[160]Ibid.

[161]President Barack Obama, "Sustaining US Global Leadership: Priorities for the 21st Century," 4.

The emergence of the aforementioned threats on Africa's Oil Coast presents AFRICOM with several challenges. Not only should the organization re-assess its current operational approach, but also examination of the command's design and structure is paramount. Organizational theorists Paul Lawrence and Jay Lorsch argue that an organizations structure should reflect the conditions it faces in the environment.[162] The patterns and events occurring across the external sectors are constantly changing and significantly influence the organization. Therefore, it is necessary for an organization to understand the different characteristics of its environment in order to function effectively and adapt to different levels of uncertainty.

After thorough assessment of AFRICOM's operational environment and examination of organizational theory, the researcher posits that the command has several structural shortfalls that require alteration to successfully accomplish its key tasks and end state. First, the organization should consider increasing its number of interagency and civil military personnel within its headquarters. The continent's growing complexity coupled with the combatant command's soft power mandate necessitates a more balanced approach to African affairs. AFRICOM's current mission set demands unified action to yield success. Since the command's formation in 2007, it has faced numerous challenges achieving unity of effort across the JIIM environment, specifically with the DOS. AFRICOM has routinely adapted its internal processes to bridge this gap and improve synchronization of continental activities. However, issues are still prevalent as many DOS individual country teams have divergent strategies that do not necessarily align with AFRICOM. As African affairs intensify additional interagency personnel and increased military coordination are necessary to achieve long-term success. The AFRICOM staff will never achieve senior policy makers intended force ratios of twenty five percent interagency personnel to seventy

---

[162]Lawrence and Lorsch, 8-13.

five percent DOD; however, to execute unified action and accomplish U.S. objectives this shortfall must be addressed.

Similarly, as the command's mission is population centric more civil military personnel are required to mitigate risk, construct effective narratives, and enhance the commanders understanding and visualization of the area of operations. AFRICOM is missing critical opportunities to gather information regarding the population and cultures inherent within African countries. The command is doing the best it can through employment of Special Operations Psychological Operations Teams to gather civil information, but the data acquired is not enough. To understand the African system, AFRICOM requires a more robust civil military presence in its headquarters and on the continent to fully appreciate the operational environment and human domain.

In addition, SECDEF Chuck Hagel's recent initiative directing combatant commands to reduce their headquarters by twenty percent poses significant challenges. As AFRICOM is already lacking sufficient specialization and personnel ratios for mission accomplishment, the organization must find innovative ways to adapt to its dynamic external environment. Through re-assessment of each staff directorate the command must identify redundancies that can mitigated through reach back to other governmental agencies. Congruently, due to the AFRICOM's headquarters location, large number of stakeholders, and vast area of operations the organization must find effective ways to execute mission command. By creation of a dynamic network structure that maximizes technological capabilities the command can truncate its size while improving collaboration and shared understanding across the JIIM environment. Holistically, the aforementioned structural changes can meet the SECDEF's guidance while simultaneously increasing critical personnel ratios to facilitate unified action.

Finally, as African conflicts continue to escalate threatening continental and international stability, AFRICOM requires more forces and resources to interact in its external environment.

The recent crisis in South Sudan offers a good case study to illustrate the researcher's hypothesis. The small non-combatant evacuation operation of American and western personnel in Juba, South Sudan required extensive AFRICOM support. The operation became interesting as four U.S. servicemen were wounded when planes they were aboard received hostile fire. Using available means AFRCIOM effectively employed elements of the RAF and SP-MAGTF in a timely manner to achieve the mission. The operation was a tremendous success for the combatant command; however, given the state of African affairs senior leaders should be concerned. As synergy increases between AQIM, Al-Shabaab, and Boko Haram coupled with the myriad of other ongoing continental crises AFRICOM may face situations it is not adequately resourced to manage. If the small South Sudan conflict consumed most of the organization's resources, imagine a synchronized terrorist attack across multiple areas.

In addition, as AFRICOM is countering extremism in the east and monitoring the Arab Spring in the north the organization's resources and forces are stretched thin. The emergence of transnational threats on Africa's Oil Coast is creating operational challenges for AFRICOM as currently constructed. Overall, since its formation the command has achieved commendable results with minimal assets throughout Africa and its Oil Coast, yet to truly be effective the command needs additional means to achieve its organizational goals. As the continent persistently changes so must AFRICOM to achieve its end state. Similarly, through modification of its operational approach and organizational structure the command can more effectively help Africans achieve a position of relative advantage while protecting vital U.S. and international interests.

Recommendations

Recommendation one is that senior U.S. policy makers and governmental officials recognize the growing importance of Africa and amplify its strategic priority. Congruently, that AFRICOM receives an increased allocation of resources to interact throughout its area of operations. Specifically, the researcher hypothesizes that the command requires additional interagency representatives, civil military personnel, military forces, and logistical support to accomplish its mission and desired end state. As LTG Terry Wolff, Director, Strategic Plans & Policy, J5 recently highlighted in a speaking engagement at Fort Leavenworth, Kansas, the United States is at a critical point regarding foreign policy. Furthermore, that the military's ability to link tactical actions to strategic ends requires innovative approaches to succeed in global affairs known as "the new normal."[163] Thus, the researcher posits that AFRICOM represents the "new normal" of a combatant command. AFRICOM's unique organizational structure, soft power mandate, and application of unified action provide the framework for the United States to maintain a position of relative advantage throughout the anticipated operational environment. However, as the organization's external environment is increasing in volatility and threatening long-term U.S. interests the command requires more inputs to achieve its desired end state. Through increased resourcing, AFRICOM can successfully adapt its organizational structure highlighting a paradigm shift for the construction of combatant commands'.[164]

Recommendation two is that due to the dynamic African system and emerging threats on the Oil Coast, AFRICOM should consider reframing the operational environment and examine options to more effectively align assets to accomplish its end state. Organizational theorist Mary Jo Hatch calls defines this as instrumental rationality or an organization's ability to achieve goals through efficient means.[165] As the interdependent problem sets on Africa's Oil Coast manifest instability threatening U.S. and global interests, AFRICOM is at a critical point regarding its strategy. The command should seek ways to improve unity of effort across the JIIM environment and attempt to formulate an operational approach that integrates and synchronizes all the

---

[163]LTG Terry Wolff, Speaker at Fort Leavenworth, Kansas, 1 December 2013.

[164]Kuhn., 10.

[165]Hatch and Cunliffe, 269.

instruments of national power to achieve synergistic effects yielding long-term impacts. The researcher posits that the Oil Coast should become AFRICOM's decisive operation as the region's problem sets directly affect long-term U.S. interests. Furthermore, using a more unified methodology, AFRICOM can achieve positive results through capacity building on the Oil Coast creating an arc of stability bolstering a model for other African nations.

Recommendation three is for AFRICOM to adapt its existing organizational structure. Due to the command's external environment and recent SECDEF guidance, AFRICOM must find innovative ways to modify its design. First, the command must maximize use of U.S. based reach back assets and streamline all of its joint staff directorates' through cutting excess personnel. Simultaneously, AFRICOM can increase its number of specialized force ratios regarding interagency and civil-military personnel. Furthermore, as the command improves mission critical personnel ratios, the organization should adopt a hybrid structure. The hybrid framework provides combinations of functional, divisional, and matrices to gain a competitive advantage. Thus, as highlighted in Figure 9, as AFRICOM decreases the size of its directorates maintaining a smaller multi-divisional form the command could maximize efficiency through consolidation of specialized personnel in a matrix style configuration to support the entire organization.

PROPOSED ORGANIZATIONAL STRUCTURE - HYBRID FORM

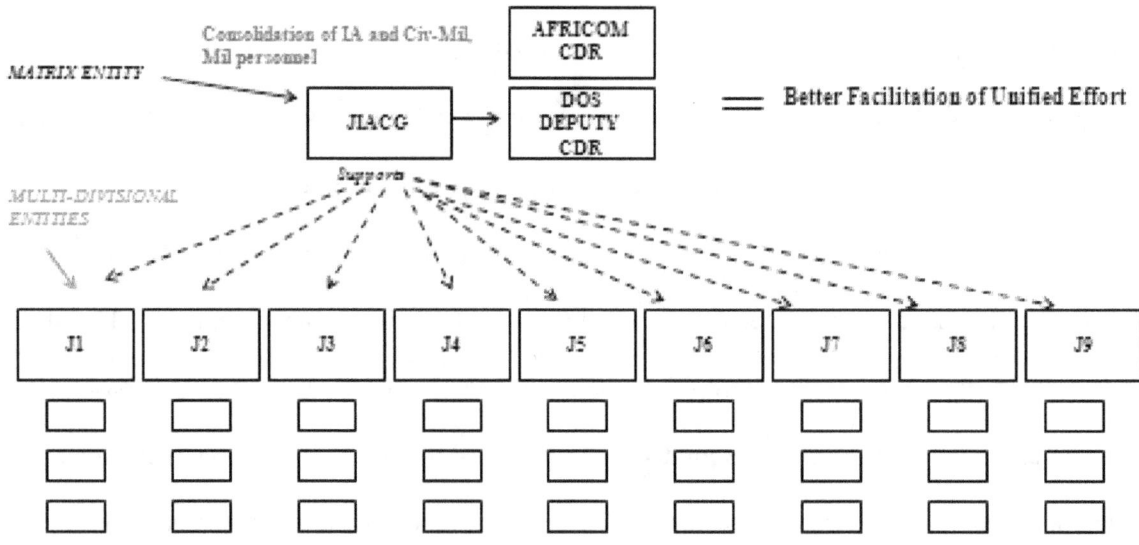

Figure 9. Proposed AFRICOM Headquarters Hybrid Design
Source: Created by author.

Specifically, to bridge the gap and better coordinate efforts across the DOS, individual

country teams, and military personnel the researcher hypothesizes that the AFRICOM

headquarters should create a joint interagency coordination group (JIACG) reporting directly to

the Deputy to the Commander for Civil-Military Activities. The JIACG is an interagency staff

group that establishes regular, timely, and collaborative working relationships between civilian

and military operational planners. The JIACG maximizes the joint force assets, coordinates the

establishment of interagency assessment teams, implements information sharing, and integrates

interagency planning processes to support long-term goals.[166] AFRICOM could maintain some

specialized interagency personnel embedded within the various staff directorates for cross

---

[166]Department of Defense, Joint Publication (JP) 3-08, *Interorganizational Coordination During Joint Operations* (Washington, DC: Government Printing Office, 2011), II-10.

functionality; however, a standalone coordination group at the headquarters level could more effectively synchronize operations and facilitate unified action. In addition, civil-military personnel would also be a part of the JIACG to integrate all aspects of the civil domain for planning and the construction of useful narratives to inform and influence the African populous.

Similarly, to help foster collaboration across the JIIM environment, specifically key African leaders and institutions, AFRICOM must enhance its dynamic network structure through the creation of an unclassified mission network. The enormous size of the command's area of operations coupled with its headquarters location requires creative solutions to execute mission command for collaboration and shared understanding.

The fourth recommendation is to provide AFRICOM with additional forces to help stabilize Africa's Oil Coast and protect vital U.S. interests. As highlighted in the earlier case study, AFRICOM faces significant challenges building continental capacity and responding to emergent crises. Specifically, as Africa's Oil Coast foments violence and instability, the command does not have adequate resources to deter threats. Thus, the organization requires another scalable and tailorable force package solely dedicated to building capacity and crisis response on the Oil Coast. The researcher hypothesizes that an additional SP-MAGTF or similar type package is paramount for AFRICOM to achieve its desired end state. Another small-scale force package with a unique composition consisting of military police, engineers, infantryman, civil affairs, maritime personnel, and interagency personnel is critical for conducting continuous security cooperation missions throughout Africa's Oil Coast. The additional force packages basing would not be on African soil, but its forward presence would facilitate the rotation of small units throughout the Gulf of Guinea to conduct military training, police training, maritime security training, infrastructure development, and governance improvement. In addition, the force could provide a crisis response element for West Africa to protect American interests. In order for AFRICOM to achieve its desired end state and accomplish President Obama's strategic goals, the command must modify its organizational structure, operational approach and acquire additional resources. The researcher's aforementioned recommendations require a lot of funding and assets during a period of fiscal constraint. However, to succeed in Africa the United States must pay it now or will pay it later. Increased U.S. capacity building efforts throughout the continent, specifically on the Oil Coast are crucial for long-term stability throughout Africa and the international system. As Carl Dolman states, "strategy is not about the first move, it is a continuous process always presenting other options."[167] Therefore, as the African environment continues to change so must AFRICOM to link tactical actions to strategic ends across time and space.

---

[167]Everett Carl Dolman, Presentation to SAMS class 14-01, 20 January 2014.

BIBLIOGRAPHY

Adegbulu, Femi. "From Guerrilla Tactics to Outright Terrorism: A Study of Boko Haram's Synergy with Al-Qaeda Terrorist Network." *The IUP Journal of International Relations* 7, no. 2 (2013): 80.

African Union. *Profile: Economic Community of West African States (ECOWAS)*, http://www.africa-union.org/root/au/recs/ECOWASProfile.pdf/ (accessed 3 January 2014).

Anderson, Sharon. "Improving Civil Affairs Planning in the African AOR." *CHIPS: The Department of Navy's Information Technology Magazine* (July 2012): 1. http://www.privacy.navy.mil/ CHIPS/ArticleDetails.aspx?id=4048/ (accessed 23 January 2014).

Axelrod, Robert, and Michael D. Cohen. *Harnessing Complexity*. Reprint. New York: Basic Books, 2001.

BBC News. "Central African Republic descending into chaos," 26 November 2013. http://www.bbc.co.uk/news/world-africa-25095471 (accessed 26 November 2013).

_____. "Nigeria's Boko Haram 'got $3m ransom' to Free Hostages," 26 April 2013, http://www.bbc.co.uk/news/world-africa-22320077/ (accessed 28 December 2013).

Bennett, Andrew, and Alexander L. George. *Case Studies and Theory Development in the Social Science*. Cambridge, MA: MIT Press, 2005.

Brown, David E. AFRICOM at 5 Years: The Maturation of a New U.S. Combatant Command. Carlisle, PA: Strategic Studies Institute, 2013.

Brownfield, William. Assistant Security of State for International Narcotics and Law EnforcementAffairs. Testimony before the Senate Caucus on International Narcotics Control, 12 March 2013.

Burton, Richard M., and Obel Børge. Strategic Organizational Diagnosis and Design: Developing Theory for Application. 2nd ed. Boston, MA: Springer, 1998.

Carson, Johnnie, Assistant Secretary of State for African Affairs. "Nigeria, One Year After Elections." 9 April 2012, 2. http://www.state.gov/p/af/rls/rm/2012/187721.htm/ (accessed 28 December 2013).

Chivvis, Christopher S., and Andrew Liepman. *North Africa's Menace: AQIM's Evolution and the U.S. Policy Response*. Santa Monica, CA: RAND Corporation, 2013, http://www.rand.org/pubs/research_reports/RR415 (accessed 27 December 2013).

Clark, Meghan. "Pirates Off West Africa's Coast Threatening African Oil, Focus Of Anti-Piracy Concerns Shifting From Horn Of Africa To West Africa." *IB Times*, November 2013, http://www.ibtimes.com/pirates-west-africas-coast-threatening-african-oil-focus-anti-piracy-concerns-shifting-horn-africa (accessed 25 November 2013).

von Clausewitz, Carl. *On War*, trans. Michael Howard and Peter Paret. Princeton University Press, 1989.

Cummings, Thomas G., and Christopher G. Worley. *Organization Development and Change*, 9th ed. Cincinnati OH; South-Western Thomson, 2008.

Daft, Richard L. *Organization Theory and Design,* 7th ed. Cincinnati, OH: South-Western Educational Publishing/Thomson, 2001.

Department of the Army. Army Doctrinal Reference Publication (ADRP) 3-0, *United Land Operations.* Washington, DC: Government Printing Office, 2012.

Department of Defense. *Counternarcotics and Global Threats Strategy.* Washington, DC: Government Printing Office, 2011.

_____. Joint Publication 3-0, *Joint Operations.* Washington, DC: Government Printing Office, 2011.

_____. Joint Publication 3-08, *Interorganizational Coordination During Joint Operations.* Washington, DC: Government Printing Office, 2011.

_____. Joint Publication 3-33, *Joint Task Force Headquarters.* Washington, DC: Government Printing Office, 2012.

_____. Joint Publication 3-37, *Civil-Military Operations.* Washington, DC: Government Printing Office, 2013.

_____. Joint Publication 5-0, *Joint Operation Planning.* Washington, DC: Government Printing Office, 2011.

Dolman, Everett Carl. *Pure Strategy: Power and Principle in the Space and Information Age (Strategy and History).* Taylor and Francis, 2004.

Etzioni, Amitai. *Modern Organizations.* Englewood Cliffs, NJ: Prentice-Hall, 1964.

Galo, Ed. "Lejeune Marines start new rotation of Special-Purpose Marine Air-Ground Task Force Africa." *Jacksonville News,* 27 January 2014. http://www.jdnews.com/jdnewstream/lejeune-marines-start-new-rotation-of-special-purpose-marine-air-ground-task-force-africa-read-more-1.268405/ (accessed 27 January 2014).

Gay, Carolyn, Department of Energy Advisor to US AFRICOM. Interviewed by author. Fort Leavenworth, Kansas. 17 December 2013.

Geopolicity. "The Economics of Piracy: Pirate Ransoms & Livelihoods off the Coast of Somalia." Geopolicity Inc., May 2011.

Gharajedaghi, Jamshid. *Systems Thinking: Managing Chaos and Complexity: A Platform for Designing Business Architecture.* New York: Elsevier, 2006, 2d edition.

Ham, Carter Gen. *2013 AFRICOM Posture Statement.* Report to Senate Armed Services Committee, Stuttgart, Germany: United States Army Africa Command, 2013.

_____. "Counterterrorism in Africa." Speech at The Homeland Security Policy Institute, 3 December 2012. http://www.gwumc.edu/hspi/events/GENHamPRF416.cfm/ (accessed 28 December 2013).

Harrison, Neil E. *Complexity in World Politics: Concepts and Methods of a New Paradigm.* New York: SUNY Press, 2006.

Hatch, Mary Jo, and Ann L. Cunliffe. *Organization Theory,* 2nd ed. Oxford: Oxford University Press, 2006.

Hodge, B.J., William P. Anthony, and Lawrence M. Gales. *Organization Theory: A Strategic Approach,* 5th ed. Upper Saddle River, NJ: Prentice Hall, 1996.

Huebschman, Mark, Deputy Chief, Counter Narcotics and Law Enforcement Division, J5, US AFRICOM. Interviewed by author. Fort Leavenworth, Kansas. 17 December 2013.

Ignatius, David. "Libyan missiles on the loose." *The Washington Post*, 8 May 2012, http://www.washingtonpost.com/opinions/libyan-missiles-on-theloose/2012/05/08/gIQA1FCUBU_story.html/ (accessed 29 December 2013).

International (ICC) Chamber of Commerce Commercial Crime Services. *Piracy falls in 2012, but seas off East and West Africa remain dangerous.*" London: ICC Commercial Crime Services, 2013, 1. http://www.icc-ccs.org/news/836-piracy-falls-in-2012-but-seas-off-east-and-west-africa-remain-dangerous-says-imb (accessed 25 November 2013).

ICC International Maritime Bureau. *Piracy And Armed Robbery Against Ships.* Annual Report 1 January – 31 December 2010. London: ICC International Maritime Bureau, 2011.

Janes World Insurgency and Terrorism. *Harakat al-Shabaab al-Mujahideen.* 4 October 2013. https://janes.ihs.com/CustomPages/Janes/DisplayPage.aspx?DocType=Reference&ItemId=+++1 320917 (accessed November 22, 2013).

_____. *Boko Haram.* 3 October 2013. https://janes.ihs.com/CustomPages/Janes/ DisplayPage. aspx?DocType=Reference&ItemId=+++1320865 (accessed 23 November 2013).

Karimi, Faith. "African pirates use millions of dollars in ransom on drugs, real estate, prostitutes." *CNN* (November 2013): 1. http://www.cnn.com/2013/11/02/world/africa/horn-of-africa-piracy-loot/ (accessed 25 November 2013).

Keenan, Jeremy. *U.S. Militarization in Africa.* Anthropology Today, 24. Oxford, England: Blackwell Publishing, 2008.

Kemp, David, CPT, Chief of Human Resources Division at US AFRICOM. Interviewed by author. Fort Leavenworth, Kansas. 17 December 2013.

Kfir, Isaac. "The Challenge that is US AFRICOM." *Joint Forces Quarterly* 49 (2008): 112. http://ndupress.ndu.edu (accessed 1 October 2013).

Killenn, Amon. U.S. Africa Command (USAFRICOM) Counter Narco-Terrorism and Law Enforcement Assistance Division. USAFRICOM, 30 September 2013.

Kuhn, Thomas S. *The Structure of Scientific Revolutions.* Chicago: University of Chicago Press, 1970.

Lawrence, Paul R., and Jay W. Lorsch. *Organization and Environment.* Boston, MA: Harvard Business Press, 1967.

Le Sage, Andre. "Non-State Security Threat in Africa: Challenges for U.S. Engagement." *PRISM Magazine* 2, no. 1 (December 2010).

Lindeman, Justine. *Global Drug Trafficking: Africa's Expanding Role.* Washington DC: Woodrow Wilson International Center for Scholars, 2009.

Lunenburg, Fred C., and Beverly J. Irby. *Writing a Successful Thesis or Dissertation: Tips and Strategies for Students in the Social and Behavioral Sciences.* Thousand Oaks, CA: Corwin, 2008.

Masters, Jonathan. "Al-Qaeda in the Islamic Maghreb (AQIM)." *Council on Foreign Relations*, 24 January 2013, 1-2, http://www.cfr.org/world/al-qaeda-islamic-maghreb-aqim/p12717/ (accessed 27 December 2013).

Morgan, David L. "A SPMAGTF is a key element for securing strategic access and partnership with African nations." *Marine Corps Gazette*. December 2012, 1. http://www.mca-marines.org/gazette/article/marine-forces-africa/ (accessed 27 January 2014).

Obama, President Barack. "U.S. Strategy for Africa," 14 June 2012, 1. http://www.whitehouse.gov/the-press-office/2012/06/14/fact-sheet-new-strategy-toward-sub saharan-africa/ (accessed 3 January 2014).

_____. *Sustaining US Global Leadership: Priorities for the 21st Century*. Defense Strategic Guidance, Washington DC: Government Printing Office, 2012.

Peralta, Eyder. "Four U.S. Service Members Injured In South Sudan." *NPR*, 21 December 2013, 1. http://www.npr.org/blogs/thetwo-way/2013/12/21/256007086/four-u-s-service-members-injured-in-south-sudan/ (accessed 27 January 2014).

Ploch, Lauren. *Nigeria: Current Issues and U.S. Policy*. Congressional Research Service, April 2013, 13, https://www.fas.org/sgp/crs/row/RL33964.pdf/ (accessed 28 December 2013).

_____. *Africa Command: U.S. Strategic Interests and the Role of the U.S. Military in Africa*. Washington, DC: Office of the Congressional Information and Publishing, 22 July 2011. www.crs.gov/ (accessed 17 January 2014).

Qatar International Academy for Security Studies. *2012 Countering Violent Extremist Report*. 13 September 2012.

Robbins, Stephen P. *Organization Theory: Structure, Design, and Applications*. Englewood Cliffs, NJ: Prentice-Hill, 1990.

Rodriguez, General David. AFRICOM's Mission and Commander's Intent, 29 July 2013, http://www.africom.mil (accessed 28 August 2013).

Said, Sammy. "Top 10 Oil Producing Countries in Africa, 2013." *The Richest* (24 April 2013): http://www.therichest.com/expensive-lifestyle/location/top-10-oil-producing-countries-in-africa-2013/ (accessed 3 January 2014).

Stewart, Scott. "Is Boko Haram More Dangerous Than Ever?" 13 December 2012, 2-4. http://www.stratfor.com/weekly/boko-haram-more-dangerous-ever (accessed 23 November 2013).

Tan, Michele. "AFRICOM: Regionally Aligned Forces Find Their Anti-terror Mission." *Defense News* (20 October 2013). http://www.defensenews.com/article/20131020/SHOWSCOUT04/310200014/ (accessed 27 January 2014).

Tharoor, Ishann. "Terror in Nairobi: Behind al-Shabab's War With Kenya." *Time* (23 September 2013), 1-2. http://world.time.com/2013/09/21/terror-in-nairobi-behind-al-shabaabs-war-with-kenya (accessed 19 November 2013).

The Africa Center for Strategic Studies. "Advancing Stability and Reconciliation in Guinea-Bissau: Lessons from Africa's First Narco-State." June 2013.

The Jamestown Foundation. "Instability in Nigeria: The Domestic Factors." 19 June 2012. https://www.cimicweb.org/cmo/compapp/Documents/docExchange/Instability_in_Nigeria-Boko_Haram_Conference_Report.pdf/ (accessed 28 December 2013).

The Soufan Group. "Boko Haram: An Increasingly Radical Threat." 19 June 2012, http://soufangroup.com/briefs/details/?Article_Id=319/ (accessed 28 December 2013).

Trelawny, Chris. "Piracy in West Africa: A symptom of wider problems?" *New African Magazine* (March 2013). London: IC Publications, 2013.

United Human Rights Council. "Genocide in Darfur." 26 November 2013. http://www.unitedhumanrights.org/genocide/genocide-in-sudan.htm (accessed 26 November 2013).

United Nations Office on Drugs and Crime. *Transnational Organized Crime in West Africa: A Threat Assessment.* February 2013.

_____. *The Transatlantic Cocaine Market.* April 2011.

_____. *Transnational Trafficking and the Rule of Law in West Africa: A Threat Assessment.* Vienna, Austria: United Nations, 2009.

_____. *World Drug Report 2013.* Vienna, Austria: United Nations 2013.

United Nations Security Council. *Resolution 1816 (2008).* 2 June 2008. http://daccess-dds-ny.un.org/doc/UNDOC/GEN/N08/361/77/PDF/N0836177.pdf?OpenElement (accessed 26 November 2013).

United States African Command. *About the Command.* http://www.africom.mil/about-the-command/ (accessed 17 January 2014).

_____. *African Contingency Operations Training and Assistance Fact Sheet.* http://www.africom.mil/what-we-do/ (accessed 29 December 2013).

_____. *Flintlock Exercise.* http://www.africom.mil/what-we-do/exercises/flintlock/ (accessed 29 December 2013).

_____. *Security Cooperation Programs.* http://www.africom.mil/what-we-do/security-cooperation-programs (accessed 26 November 2013).

_____. *Transcript: General Rodriguez on Security Cooperation in Sub-Saharan Africa.* Washington, DC, 25 October 2013, 1-2. http://www.africom.mil/Newsroom/Transcript/11406/general-rodriguez-on-security-cooperation-in-sub-saharan-africa/ (accessed 29 December 29 2013).

U.S. Army Europe Command. 21st Theater Sustainment Brigade. http://www.eur.army.mil/21TSC/mission.asp/ (accessed 29 January 2014).

United States Department of State. *National Counterterrorism Center: Country Reports on Terrorism 2011.* 31 July 2012. http://www.state.gov/j/ct/rls/crt/2011/195555.htm (accessed 19 November 2013).

_____. Bureau of International Narcotics and law Enforcement Affairs. The West Africa Cooperative Security Initiative: A Shared Partnership, 3 July 2012, 1. http://www.state.gov/ documents/organization/166329.pdf/ (accessed 2 January 2014).

United States Energy Information Association. *Angola Country Analysis Brief.* 30 December 2013. http://www.eia.gov/countries/country-data.cfm?fips=AO/ (accessed 3 January 2014.

_____. *Nigeria Country Analysis Brief,* 30 December 2013, http://www.eia.gov/countries/country-data.cfm?fips=NI/ (accessed 3 January 2014).

_____. *Top World Oil Producers, 2012,* http://www.eia.gov/countries/index.cfm/ (accessed 3 January 2014).

United States Government. Interagency Strategy. *West Africa Cooperative Security Initiative (WACSI)*. November 2011.

United States House of Representatives Committee on Homeland Services. *Boko Haram: Growing Threat to the U.S. Homeland*, 13 September 2013, 20. http://homeland.house.gov/sites/homeland.house.gov/files/documents/09-13-13-Boko-Haram-Report.pdf/ (accessed 28 December 2013).

University of Maryland. *Global Terrorism Database*. http://www.start.umd.edu/gtd (accessed 19 November 2013).

Vandiver, John Vandiver "South Sudan crisis lands Marine crisis response unit its largest mission." *Stars and Stripes*, 24 December 2013. http://www.stripes.com/news/south-sudan-crisis-lands-marine-crisis-response-unit-its-largest-mission-1.259075/ (accessed 27 January 2014).

Van Evera, Stephen. *Guide to Methods for Students of Political Science*. (Ithaca: Cornell University Press, 1997.

Volman, Daniel. "Why America wants military HQ in Africa." *New African Magazine*, 2008.

Weisberger, Marcus. "DoD Begins Cutting Staff Sizes, Will Reorganize Policy Office." *Defense News*, (5 December 2013): 1. http://www.defensenews.com/article/20131205/DEFREG02/312050012/DoD-Begins-Cutting-Staff-Sizes-Will-Reorganize-Policy-Office/ (accessed 28 January 2014).

Wyler, Liana Wyler, and Nicolas Cook. *Drug Trafficking in West Africa: Background and Possible Questions for an Upcoming Hearing*. Washington, DC: Office of the Congressional Information and Publishing, 8 May 2012.

Yamamoto, Don. *Instability in Africa*. Report to House of Foreign Affairs. Washington DC: Department of State, 2012.